ACT, REST, RESET, REPEAT

Create Change Without Burning Out

By Katie Hodgetts

Act, Rest, Reset, Repeat
Katie Hodgetts

First published in the UK and USA in 2026 by Watkins,
an imprint of Watkins Media Limited, Unit 11, Shepperton House,
83–89 Shepperton Road, London N1 3DF

enquiries@watkinspublishing.com

Editorial Director: Ella Chappell
Commissioning Editor: Sophie Blackman
Editorial Assistant: Caitlin Nolan
Typeset by Lapiz
Head of Design: Karen Smith
Head of Production: Uzma Taj

Typeset in Minon Variable Concept & Haboro Serif
Printed and bound by CPI Group (UK) Ltd, Croydon, CR0 4YY

The manufacturer's authorised representative in the EU for product safety is: eucomply OÜ – Pärnu mnt 139b-14, 11317 Tallinn, Estonia, hello@eucompliancepartner.com, www.eucompliancepartner.com

A CIP record for this book is available from the British Library

ISBN: 978-1-83681-025-4 (Paperback)
ISBN: 978-1-83681-030-8 (eBook)

10 9 8 7 6 5 4 3 2 1
www.watkinspublishing.com

For Benjamin, whose love is my armour.
And Judy Bryan, who taught me that all of it was possible.

CONTENTS

PART ONE

CHAPTER 1: THE PERMACRISIS

"The greatest danger of our time is the deadening of our response."[1]

Joanna Macy and Chris Johnstone, *Active Hope*

Let's be real. We are burned out. Anxious. Disillusioned. Many of us want to help nurture a world in crisis, but the sheer scale of injustice, environmental breakdown and political chaos has left us overwhelmed and overloaded. Globalization of the 20th century promised prosperity and unity, yet we have grown up in a world with widening inequality and fraying global solidarity. At the time of writing, there are 59 large-scale conflicts happening in the world, a figure that has increased by 60–90 per cent over the past two decades.[2] What some now call the *permacrisis* – the "dizzying sense of lurching from one unprecedented event to another" – captures this well, as we wonder bleakly what new horrors might be around the corner.[3] With each event arriving before we've had time to process the last, we can feel breathless. We were promised a life of more beauty than this.

While global crises escalate, community-level engagement has thinned in many Western societies. We spend less time with our grandparents and in community spaces. We sharpen our morality less through scripture or intergenerational wisdom and more through 60-second reels and TikToks. All contribute to the loneliness epidemic. In the UK, almost 50 per cent of 18–24-year-old women identify as lonely.[4] There is a sense that collectively we are experiencing *the degradation of the soul* – the spiritual, moral and social fracturing of ourselves in relation to others and Life. Yes, we were promised a life of more beauty than this . . . And we can still find it.

To transform the world, we first need to transform how we "do" changemaking. A different way of enacting change is not only possible, but it is necessary. I began changemaking with a laser-focus on action, but the deeper I went, the more I realized that external action alone isn't enough for the long term. Not when burnout is becoming the norm. A paradigm shift is needed, one where engaging with climate justice or mental health or human rights doesn't lead to inertia but enlivenment; where caring about the world doesn't *temporarily* let in connection, care and kinship but creates an open-door policy.

There is a carousel of emotions that come with peering at the destruction of ecosystems, countries, Indigenous lands and livelihoods. To name but a few, you might resonate with the feelings of sadness, disbelief, anxiety, burnout, exhaustion, despair, rage, anger, resignation, hopelessness, frustration, loneliness, betrayal and insanity. You might swing between some of these emotions from hour to hour, minute to minute, or you might feel some of them at the same time. When we see headlines like "searches for climate anxiety increase by 73 times" we might understand why.[5] Because it's shit scary, and somewhere deep down (maybe buried really deep down for some), we're all a little bit shit scared.

You might also cope by going into denial, which has many guises. Sometimes it is not suggesting that these horrors aren't happening, rather that denial can be non-engagement. We are living through a truly unsettling period of human history, where your TikTok feed will take you straight from a funny cat video to a trending dance to a dead child in a conflict zone. Sometimes we choose to scroll. Sometimes our hearts cannot hold the grief of the world first thing in the morning. Sometimes boundaries around when we engage and when we don't become less about virtue-signalling and more about safeguarding our capacity. In small and controlled doses, denial can be a helpful coping mechanism – perhaps you even skim read the first few paragraphs of this book? But in larger bouts and extrapolated to larger populations, denial and apathy have become two widespread emotions that are stifling progress. While denial and apathy are a privileged and dangerous choice, I understand them. Like my ex-colleague once said, social change is just "too depressing" to engage with. To thwart the deadening of our response, there is an increasing mandate to enliven our approach and our changemaking too.

Act, Rest, Reset, Repeat: Act

I began changemaking when I was 21, concerned primarily with the "Act" portion of this formula. I devoted myself to different campaigns and believed that change hinged on questions regarding action alone. Do we need electric cars or does their production exacerbate exploitative resource extraction? How can I limit my lifestyle emissions alongside my campaign work? Can AI be our saviour in finding a climate-emissions solution? What legislation is required? A salary ceiling? What does a Green New Deal paradigm look like? How can we push for legislative and societal change? As we balance on the brink of collective ruin, how we act and what we do will be the pressing features of our generation. What is required is a whole generation of changemakers, pushing in different areas of society for different solutions at local, national and international level. Yet staggering rates of burnout and fatigue are not only eroding the spirit of activism but are compromising our ability to act for the long haul. If we are to move beyond a "Feel helpless? Then do more" prognosis, we need to build our awareness of the deep psychological, interpersonal and spiritual barriers that can make taking climate or any social justice action unsustainable.

After ten years in the sector, I recognize that our obsession with external action alone could be part of the problem. What feels more important to me – and is the basis for this book and my work – is shifting *human capacity* to the centre of attention, with action the byproduct. If revolutionary change lies in the ingenuity, empowerment and perseverance of common citizens, then my question has changed from "what is the right action and how do we take it?" to "how do we activate and sustain a generation of changemakers?" Because human-centred activism is activism in its most alive form.

Human-centred activism is activism in its most alive form.

In considering human capacity, we first need to design a new blueprint for changemaking that centres on sustainability – not the kind of sustainability that counts our emissions or recycles our placards (though that's great). This is one of sustainability of the self, not just sustainability of the planet – the *psychological* and *emotional* sustainability that makes it possible to keep going for a lifetime, not just a season. To take the hits like soil takes rain. To develop an ability for emotional alchemy, transforming concern into courage. *This* is how we shift activism from a project we take on, to a posture we move from. Moreover, if we need agents of change across every level of society on multiple different fronts, then changemaking needs to become not the plight of a few, but an obligation and possibility for everyone. This includes your anarchist housemates, your school friends from home and yes, your nan. Our blueprint should redefine changemaking to make it more accessible, enjoyable, diverse and impactful, celebrating all forms of engagement, not just protests, and weaving in joy and extending the invitation to others. Perhaps *that's* how I get my ex-colleague involved.

Another facet of human capacity is how we bounce back if we are burned out, a plight so many of us have experienced. Burnout, though highly complex and personal, is commonly associated with fatigue or tiredness. There is a heaviness that settles into your bones, a weariness so deep it can pin you to your bed or make the smallest task disproportionately overwhelming. But what I've come to see across the board is that burnout is about more than "tiredness". Perhaps you're not tired. Perhaps you're *impoverished.* Perhaps you've become so absorbed by your cause that you've dimmed the lights on what you love. Perhaps you are impoverished in spirit, inspiration, connection and joy. That's why a walk in fresh air, a plunge in cold water or the embrace of an old friend can feel so unexpectedly restorative. Placing human capacity at our centre is the route back to being ourselves. After all, it is a balanced you – your gifts, vitality and wisdom – that will drive lasting change.

"So, how do we do this?" has become my obsession. How do we revitalize changemaking as a pursuit associated with collective joy and the reweaving of community, rather than loneliness, restriction and burnout? How do we reapproach changemaking in a way that also addresses the mental health crisis? How do we unlock and preserve the latent power of humans without burning them out? How do we "save the planet" – and feel good doing it? Is that even possible? These questions became the starting curiosities for the organization I would set up aged 24, The Resilience Project, which would grow into a global organization.

Rest: Distress to De-stress

If to act is to declare *this matters,* to rest is to remember *so do I.* Rest is an integral part of changemaking, though we aren't taught how to do it. It is sometimes associated with mindless social media scrolling and binge-watching *Desperate*

> If to act is to declare *this matters,* to rest is to remember *so do I.*

Housewives (at which I'm proficient), as if rest is something you need to earn. Other times it is seen as exclusive to the wellness sector, as if rest is something you need to buy. Under these guises rest becomes mental inertia or physical abandon. Rest has more flavour, vibrancy and wisdom than the passivity of the armchair. It is more than moving from a place of distress to de-stress. Rest is where we find truth, in the mind, body and nervous system. If busyness and productivity are concerned with "what's next", rest is concerned with "what is". It is a state of physiological and psychological quietening, where both consciously and unconsciously we convert our experiences into learning, uncover realizations and are offered a different pathway forward. Stillness brings truth: we pause to feel, not to retreat.

I am fanatical about rest going beyond bathtubs, foot spas and wellbeing. While this book will undoubtedly find a home in the "self-care and wellbeing" section, let it be clear from the outset: I don't want or expect you simply to be well. When we make "wellness" our main aspiration, any deviation feels like a failure or a regression. Internalizing wellness as the goal makes it easier to vilify sadness, anger and malaise. Moving from a state of "well" to "worked up" can be regarded as a mark of inadequacy. This becomes especially pronounced in the changemaking space where grappling with big, complex emotions is part of the territory. But deviations from well hold great value. For example, there is value in feeling so inspired by the world that you throw back the curtains to your soul. There is great value in being outraged by the things you see around you and the systems that perpetuate harm and exploitation. Tended to properly, these emotional deviations are great catalysts to act. They aren't to be suppressed, hidden or shamed, but understood, befriended and utilized.

Indeed, I want you to be both heartbroken by the losses we face and enlivened by our victories. Because the truth is the world will not be transformed by wellness alone. Many Western wellbeing trends exist to nullify sensation and minimize the discomfort of "strong" emotions. An unspoken emotional hierarchy is created, where peace, calm and serenity are upheld as the highest ideals, while emotions like anger, cynicism and scepticism are treated as computational errors to be corrected. The mantra of "good vibes only" may work to maintain a surface-level semblance of wellness in the short term, but it fails to honour the deeper currents of sadness and pain, which exist in us all. While I understand the sentiment that peace starts with each of us, that's not where it ends. It ends with justice, redistribution, healing and change. Mindfulness and balance are essential, but it's emotional abundance and emotional variety that I'm going to convince you will force personal and planetary progress.

Befriending, rather than rejecting, our vast emotional terrain opens space for the lessons that seemingly unpalatable emotions like rage and cynicism have to offer us. Navigating and sifting through this complex tangle of emotions – climate anxiety, intergenerational betrayal, despair, hope – the journey will undoubtedly make pitstops at wellness. While standing in the pain and suffering of the world might be antithetical to being well, I hope I can offer morsels of stories, evidence and text to guide you to *finding* wellness – not passive well-being but active well-finding. Wellness then becomes a by-product, rather than the focus.

Reset: From Self-care to Self-change

We then move from rest to reset. To reset is not to start again now that you're not tired, but to understand why you became so tired in the first place and make the necessary changes: the process of installing the updates, identifying the bugs and rebooting the system. It is less about self-care and more about self-change. The terms "self" and "change" are both misleading here. First of all, "self" could imply that the burden is on you. If *you* change, the *world* will change. While I agree with that in part, what truly needs to change is much, much bigger than you – systems, structures and trajectories as well as legislation and elected politicians need to change. Second, while change happens within the individual, we're not doing it alone. It is catalysed by community. The process is about the individual, though the work must be done collectively, which is why peer support plays a central role in our reset.

To reset requires more than a yoga class. It requires us to engage deeply with the collective and internalized narratives that might lock us into cycles of boom and bust. This might involve looking at communities we've found ourselves in and seeing if they're propping up systems of harm or dismantling them. Or we might have to be honest with how we relate to our self-worth, and whether we consciously or unconsciously tie it to productivity. To reset is to turn our gaze counterintuitively from the external turmoil to our internal landscape and the strength of our social connectivity. This is not an invitation to stop pushing for systemic, legislative and discursive change, but realizing that without adequate internal resourcing we are likely to stifle the creative and long-term thinking required for success. It's in the interplay between internal activation and external activism that resilience is found.

Resilience is how we weather storms, not the absence of storms. The absence of storms is toxic positivity, outlandish optimism or sheer denial. Resilience, on the other hand, is how (not how quickly) we bounce back from difficulty, and how in adversity we may not become buried but planted. As a concept, resilience isn't binary. One isn't either resilient or not. It's not a skill we acquire for life or a destination we reach. Resilience is a practice, rather than a given state, shaped by intention, identity and community. Just like a river, which runs wide and sometimes narrow, our sense of resilience will meander in response to our changing internal and external landscape, our levels of support and our position within the world. Over time, some streams will deviate from a river, depleting our stores, while at other points streams join the river, adding to its strength and power. Some things, like mutual aid, feelings of safety or climbing a mountain, will add to how resilient we feel. Others, like financial instability, grief of loved ones or systemic oppression, will detract from it.

> Resilience is a practice, rather than a given state, shaped by intention, identity and community.

If the goal is resilience rather than wellness, reset – or self-change – becomes central. Self-change guides us in understanding the patterns that don't serve us or our activism, and to acknowledge and honour the work we've already done to bolster ourselves. Change is uncertain and unsteady by its very nature, so changing the world will be unsteady too. And changing ourselves – our narratives, our relationship to our emotions, our understanding of burnout, our understanding of who we are – might be a little messy as well. But that doesn't mean that it's not the most gratifying adventure of your life: to truly know and accept yourself.

Repeat: A Rhythm Not a Regression

Repeat is an important part of this formula because healing, growth and resilience are not linear journeys. We may recover from a bout of burnout only to feel it happening all over again. Developing our sense of resilience does not make us immune to burnout, but it arms us with the learning and wisdom to enable us to make a quicker or more gracious recovery. It is likely that you will feel burned out more than once, because life is full of stress. Campaigns fail. A fascist is elected. Our loved ones get sick. Repeat is a life-long journey of an unknown number of repetitions.

I know this from my own journey. In 2019 I burned out from climate campaigning, resolute in the aftermath to learn enough about it to prevent it in others. Two years later, I was running residentials and workshops on resilience and burnout. I had assumed that made me resistant to it. When I received some devastating family news later that year, I realized that learning about resilience won't keep you safe from pain. Here I discovered the wisdom that not just campaigning, but *Life* itself is a journey of Acting, Resting, Resetting and Repeating.

Climate Activation

Act, Rest, Reset, Repeat has been written to consolidate the learnings of a decade in activism, the "youthquake" of the 2019 climate movement and over half a decade building an organization – The Resilience Project – which explores with young changemakers how we take action without burning out. It was established in 2020 and I have since spent each year at The Resilience Project designing, delivering and weaving youth-led spaces for peer support, inner development and intergenerational mentoring. All of our work is underscored by our Climate Activation model, an inner-led, peer support learning journey facilitated in youth-led space. It has been designed by psychologists and youth activists and its impact researched by Dr Britt Wray (Stanford University) and Dr Emma Lawrence and Daniella Watson (Imperial College, London). It is becoming increasingly recognized that positive social impact hinges not only on policy change but on personal reckoning with the inner dimensions of change. Simply put, Climate Activation is a model to facilitate this inner-led journey, which happens in community over eight weeks, to build our self-awareness, levels of connectedness and feelings of hope as a strategy for world change.

Note that activation differs from activism. While history is a written account of activism changing the world, the imagery of activism has shifted in the last few years from Parks, the Suffragettes and Stonewall to superglue, disruption and crime. The word "activism" has become intentionally sullied by both the media and governments, reducing public support for activism, and making our movement seem less about community and more about criminality. Whereas activism is an event or campaign wedded to outcomes and impact, activation is a journey involving discoveries and learning. Taking action, in all its manifest forms, becomes a *by-product* of climate activation. The model runs so that we don't know what kind of action we'll be designing or taking after moving through the eight weeks – nor do we prescribe it – but it will be one underscored by self-knowing, imagination, support, care and inspiration.

Each year we train a small cohort of young climate leaders across the world to host these eight-week communities of care and belonging, which we call "Resilience Circles". These circles meet weekly to talk candidly about the realities of the polycrisis, explore resilience-building practices and to build a new constellation of care and kinship, rather than competition. Our community-led model means that Resilience Circles are specific to movements, geographies or shared lived experience, hence we've established Circles for young People of Colour, Queer+ folk and COP27 campaigners. Through working with thousands of young activists, holding interventions in 25 different countries, our work celebrates "depth" over "breadth". All of our programmes, from youth-led book groups to mindfulness programmes to Resilience Circles, run between eight weeks and nine months to facilitate the long and often difficult work of change – something the urgency narrative of our crises held us back from doing.

I admit up front that I'm not a psychologist. I was a youth climate activist who campaigned and mobilized over 80,000 people onto the streets for climate justice. Setting up The Resilience Project in my early twenties grew out of my own story of burnout and a growing unease with the dynamics I witnessed in the youth climate movement. There was exceptional talent, but also in-fighting, toxicity and the deep currents of the existing societal legacies of racism, colonialism and patriarchy. I witnessed the glorification of burnout and a kind of internal collapse that mirrored the very systems we were resisting. We were losing ourselves in our "activist" label and burning more bridges than we were building. It was clear to me that while we championed being "anti-capitalist" and "feminist", the learned teachings of these systems, such as ego, individualism and competition, still played out in our groups. Sound familiar?

Exploring a more human-centred activism has been my passion for ten years: progressing from establishing a "Wellbeing Officer" for various youth movements age 21, to scaling The Resilience Project and our Activation model from the UK to Europe and East Africa. Activation brings all the human facets of changemaking to the foreground. It begins at the heart – understanding the vast emotional terrain of change – to root us in our "why". It's not a healing journey, but a "*whole*ing" journey, to help us better understand, appreciate and value all of what and who we are – even the less light and bright bits. It says that this too is welcome here. The anger, rage and disappointment and longings. It progresses to the realm of the mind (cognition, culture, consciousness) and highlights the narratives we subscribe to which may limit our capacity as changemakers. Then beyond us, it works to build a strong, caring community, with peer support as the keystone for sustainable change. Finally, we explore a holistic approach to taking action, which isn't just something exclusively "out there", but rather is to live as though another world is not only possible but is already unfolding through us.

How to Use This Book

While this book moves through eight tangible themes that align with the eight-week Climate Activation model, this is not an "eight-step guide to ultimate resilience". There are no hacks to changing the world or changing your life. There is only deep work where the cost is our time, but the reward is our truth. Appreciating that resilience cannot be bought or read but lived and unlocked, reframes this book as a guidebook rather than as an instruction manual. All eight chapters in Part Two feature at least one exercise that is explored in our Climate Activation model. While the focus was specifically on climate, the guideposts have been expanded to speak to all forms of changemaking, because the 21st century is calling for our work to feel more interconnected. I encourage you to engage with these exercises in pairs or groups. You may want to find a group to work through the chapters with and build your own Resilience Circle. Though it may be tempting to skip these exercises, I implore you to engage with them. Resilience is an active practice and though we can read about it and intellectualize it, its staying power stems from how we metabolize it into our bodies.

> Resilience cannot be bought or read but lived and unlocked.

The research conducted by Imperial College London found that Resilience Circles are proven to significantly improve emotional wellbeing, support the navigation of complex emotions, strengthen emotional and collective resilience and identify helpful self-care tools.[6] The chapters in this book are inspired by this validated approach, the stories of many participants and the work informed by young people across six continents. However, what I speak of here may not necessarily reflect your own experience. I invite you to take what is helpful from this book and iterate the model in your own communities in the way that feels most authentic, because we need fewer gurus and more community. While the model's effectiveness has been demonstrated by mixed-method studies, I must stress that like all models, it is non-exhaustive and fallible. It has been inspired largely by US and European thinking and institutions from the Global North, hence it may not capture the spirit of other parts of the world. That said, we have tested parts with international youth and found that the essence remains the same across borders: changemakers need places to be heard and understood, to share all the "arrghs" and "eeks" of modern life and find spaces of genuine connection where they are loved and feel worthy as a human first, a changemaker second. I wrote this book as a love letter to those hungry for change, in the hope that they would see their pain and confusion mirrored back to them and know they're not alone.

Part One traces the emotional and theoretical underpinnings of the Climate Activation model, detailing my own experiences of powerful action and my resulting burnout during the 2019 Greta Thunberg-inspired "Youthquake". It explains the concept of "*inner*tersectional changemaking" and how a renewed emphasis on our individual inner landscape can contribute to stronger collective units. Part Two introduces the Climate Activation model itself, moving through the eight guideposts for taking action without burning out. Grounded in psychology, it answers big questions on pushing for change. For example, how do we avoid burnout? What is the rich variety of rest I've alluded to? What can we gain from embracing our anger and is there space for joy and fun? (Spoiler alert: absolutely.) Finally, Part Three explores the notion of "Repeat", which considers how we can unlock resilience and come back to it time and time again, citing my own experiences of repeat emotional collapse. There is great irony and richness that writing extensively about burnout has not made me immune to it. Part Three also looks at my second burnout in light of my sibling's cancer diagnosis, and the powerful reminder than the personal is deeply interwoven with the political. The person standing behind a cause is very much still that: a person. What we endure and unearth from strife and challenge can offer morsels of learning to our changemaking efforts, and vice versa.

A Note on Language

Throughout this book I use the terms "eight-week model" and "Climate Activation model" interchangeably. I also use terminology to delineate peoples and geographies, including but not limited to the Global North and the Global South to distinguish between geographies, and MAPA (most affected people and areas) as a group of peoples. MAPA highlights the disproportionate impacts of climate change on certain communities and regions. It underscores the reality that those who have contributed least to the climate crisis, such as Indigenous peoples and low-lying island nations and communities, are often the most severely affected by its consequences. I anticipate that as all language does, it will shift and change to better define the people it represents. I use the term "Global Majority" to refer to Indigenous people, people of African, Asian or Latin American descent, as they constitute approximately 85 per cent of the world's population – far from a minority. I intentionally use the word "changemaking" more so than "activism". Words carry power and my choice for changemaking stresses the importance of change as well as action, Reset as well as Act. By using changemaking, which is wider in its remit, I hope to invite in those beyond climate and those who feel "activist" isn't a label that represents them. Imposter syndrome stopped me from self-identifying as an "activist" for years. In using "changemaker", I say to those somewhere on the spectrum of taking action and to those who care deeply about positive change: I see you. I will also refer to spirituality. Please don't confuse this with crystals etc. By spirituality, I am referring to the "non-material" – for example feelings such as love, connection, inspiration and interconnectedness – as opposed to the "material", by which I mean tangible things such as clothes, cars or physical protests.

This book will not instruct you how to deliver a campaign, but it might inspire you to do so. Through the guideposts outlined, I endeavour to shine a light on how to transform yourself into an empowered changemaker for the long term, with mental fitness at the centre. This offers a different approach to leadership in the polycrisis, where the solution to avoiding burnout is not to feel less but to feel *more*: specifically, more aliveness. Because numbness is understandable, but aliveness is revolutionary. My hope is that it will transform the eco-worrier, the eco-resigned, the eco-angry and the eco-it's-too-fucking-late into the eco-empowered, the eco-engaged and the eco-alive. I'm not asking you to change the way you live, to stop going on holiday or to glue yourself to trees (but that's a bonus). I am inviting you to come with me and explore the deep, inner and collective transformation the 21st century requires of us: a paradigm shift so we live fuller, more connected, enriched lives while honouring planetary boundaries. This version of changemaking is not just about the output but about the path itself. Because when we engage from a place that is grounded, supported and connected, something powerful happens: we don't just avoid burnout, we start to uncover larger versions of ourselves. Changemaking stops being something we *do* and becomes part of how we *are* in the world.

The solution to avoiding burnout is not to feel less but to feel *more*.

CHAPTER 2:

THE KIDS ARE NOT ALRIGHT

It was COP26, the world's largest annual climate conference. For two weeks, delegates and leaders from nearly 200 countries gathered to hammer out global climate targets. In 2021, the conference took place in Glasgow, and I was inside the event space as a youth delegate representing the youth-led group, UK Youth Climate Coalition (UKYCC).

Our team of eight had spent the past year meticulously planning for this moment. We met online every Tuesday evening, dissecting updates, strategizing our campaigns and dreaming about how we might leave a mark on this historic event. We were young, 18 to 25, unpaid, driven entirely by the urgency of our mission. After over a year of lockdown, COP26 felt like a watershed moment for the future of climate action.

In Glasgow, our plans included demonstrations both inside and outside of the conference: calling out greenwashing, exposing how Big Oil continued to fund parts of the event and demanding accountability from those in power. But one opportunity stood out from the rest: a closed-door meeting with Miriam, a senior official in the United Nations Framework Convention on Climate Change (UNFCCC) Secretariat – the governing body of the entire COP process. This was the woman who could influence negotiations on a global scale. If we could inspire even a flicker of ambition in her, we might – just might – be able to ripple that energy through the conference. No pressure, right?

We spent the afternoon before the meeting scrounging free coffee and preparing a long list of questions, including: "How are you preparing to act on Loss and Damage?" "What ambitions do you have for the Nationally Determined Contributions?" "Will negative emissions technologies be featured in the final text? We peppered each question with acronyms to camouflage our age, masking our anxiety with intellectualism. It was an exceptional and rare opportunity, so we wanted to feel as ready as possible.

The time came and we shimmied into a small room overlooking the pavilion. I was in my early twenties, wearing my best (and only) suit, my scraggle of hair pulled back into a tight bun. A smartly dressed woman sat down, smiling at us. After a moment of shuffling papers and clearing her throat, Miriam asked us to begin. We'd rehearsed this, we knew who was asking what, but as a youth campaigner I only wanted to scream, "WHY AREN'T WE ACTING?" and bang my fists against the wall. What came out of my mouth was in fact a timid question about the UK's position within the climate negotiations. Did I understand the answer she gave? Not really. But I nodded with appreciation to avoid disturbing the balance of the room.

Every question we asked felt like it was bouncing off an invisible barrier of diplomacy. Her answers were polished, vague and impersonal, designed to fill the silence without offering any real substance. Were our questions as equally confusing? We asked her if the negotiations looked like we would be hitting our country's climate targets. "Well, it's quite difficult to say." She barely blinked. "There are a lot of moving parts to be considered. It remains to be seen what will come out of these negotiations." I nodded. We moved onto our next question. That's how the next 30 minutes proceeded.

As we steamrolled through our list, it felt like the room had become a vacuum for inspiration, hope and tenacity, three things that I felt the youth movement embodied. The sterile atmosphere of the room clashed violently with the raw urgency I'd felt every single day as a youth climate campaigner. For years, we'd marched, rallied and fought to be heard. We'd faced harassment, threats of violence and burnout, yet we kept going because we believed we could make a difference. And here we were, face to face with one of the most powerful people in the process, and it felt like nothing we said could penetrate the bureaucratic wall around her. Perhaps COP26 was not the ellipsis between the youth uprising, lockdown and our new beginning … Perhaps it was the full stop.

The carefully crafted façade I had put on – the suit, the rehearsed questions, the polite demeanour – began to feel like a betrayal of what we stood for. In almost 30 years this was the only COP to take place in the UK and who knew when the next one would be. So, just like Greta Thunberg in 2019, when she skipped school to sit outside of the Swedish parliament to protest a lack of climate education, I decided it was time to go off-script.

"Miriam," I interrupted, taking a deep breath to steady myself. "Thank you for taking the time to talk us through your answers." I moved my hands to my lap to hide their shaking. I told myself to keep going, you've started now, the balance isn't just disturbed – it's turbulent. Don't stop.

"I need you to level with me, honestly." I could feel the silence changing shape in the room, becoming tense and fraught. Half of my team stared in disbelief, the others masking encouraging smiles.

"I have spent the last two years in the youth strike movement. Our small team has spent weekends and evenings designing marches for tens of thousands of people. We've lost sleep over the violent threats we've received. In Bristol, we received Facebook messages that men were going to drive their diesel cars through the marches to hit people. We've had to learn about safe crowd management, installing safety barriers to manage stampedes, navigating accessibility, PR, media conduct and interviews, when all we ever wanted was a safe future. We've been told that we're inspiring, yet we've seen absolutely no action we've inspired. We've been told that we're the future, but we seem unable to impact the present. We've been told that we are public heroes – unless we cause traffic problems and then we are public nuisances. We are all between the ages of 13 and 23. Most of us are medicated for anxiety. All we ever wanted was to be young and safe. We called on adults to protect us and you failed."

For a moment, I braced myself for dismissal – for a curt, calculated response that would shut me down. But instead, something shifted in Miriam's demeanour. The polished veneer melted away, replaced by something I hadn't expected. Sorrow. It seemed like she'd moved from an intellectual space to an emotional understanding. She could see and relate to the care buried within my words. And she cared too. Somehow my shift to emotions broke down the difference in our ages and the cost of our suits. It brought us all together in this room under one banner and into a dialogue rather than an interrogation. At that moment we knew we were on the same team.

"You must tell me," I went on. "Because I'm exhausted. Have we made any impact outside of the streets we shout into? Has this all been in vain?"

She shuffled in her seat, looking at her hands. She was taking a pause, clearly deciding how much of the professional veil to peel back and how much to stick to the organizational line. I am so grateful, to this day, for her courage in lifting the mask.

"Thank you for your comments." She paused. "I can't really put into words the impact the youth strikes have had on the COP negotiations. A few years back, the negotiation room had one wall that was entirely glass. People could see in, but importantly we could see out. We had a direct view outside of the building to the street down below. It so happened that down below on an integral day of negotiating, thousands of young people were marching outside." Her tone softened.

"We saw young people calling us in on their future and it changed the nature of those negotiations. It grounded us, reminded us of the possibility of our work. You were a thousand-person reminder of why we made choices in our lives to be sat here, doing what we are doing. You reminded us of the ambitions we held in our youth for justice and equity that may have been lost along the way. I can't really find the words, but if I had to choose them, I would say that youth climate action has raised ambition in a way I've never seen before in my career."

In a way she'd never seen before. All because we went outside and did something. Because we took a stand. The power of youth marching together is more than the policy change we're calling for. It's a statement. A reminder to adults of what they'd once believed in – or still do. The youth strikers not only stamped their feet on the floor but their mark in history.

That experience is something I think about often, almost half a decade later. Firstly, it taught me that "winning" is not always about policy change or campaign goals but about shifting hearts and minds. It may be harder to distil into an infographic, but it has been the seed of historic change. It influences cultural norms, consumer habits and it is the crucial precondition for wider legislative shift. Being unable to see, hold or quantify your efforts does not make them obsolete. They may be contributing to a greater, wider stirring.

Secondly, real dialogue was unlocked in that boardroom not through facts or figures, but from a candid retelling of my own experience. Showcasing this vulnerability did not hamper discussions as traditional negotiation handbooks may suggest but furthered them. Sarah Jaquette Ray, author of *A Field Guide to Climate Anxiety*, touches on this idea with "climate wisdom", defined as "the understanding that our ability to respond to climate change and to work on climate justice issues is shaped more by our emotional selves than by our rational selves. The sooner we make that connection, the more effective we'll be".[7]

Climate change is, at its core, an unfolding story of collective vulnerability: from the fragility of ecosystems to the uprooting of accustomed ways of life to the futures we dare to imagine. If the crisis itself is so human, so tender in its stakes, then why is it met with cold rationality or sterile debate? To speak openly about our fears, our grief, our desires, is not a barrier to meaningful discussion but a bridge. Vulnerability is the bridge between facts and feelings, data and hearts. Like my meeting with Miriam, vulnerability reveals what is true and raw within us, inviting others to care and act. This remarkable experience planted an important seed in my mind. If civil society momentum was waning, in part due to the toll of screaming into the void, perhaps this moment was a calling for a paradigm shift in how we "do" changemaking. A calling to again go off-script.

When the Marches End

There is enormous power and potential in the first part of this book's title – *Act*. The mobilization of ordinary people has resulted in boycotts, legislative change and shifting cultural norms. Independence movements, civil rights campaigns and human rights defenders have remapped nations and pulled entire demographics into conversations about justice. It was the very mobilization of the Suffragettes in the early 20th century and the rise of rights for women that paved the way for me to be able to write this book. In the climate space, contemporary action from ordinary individuals can be tracked back to the 1960s. Greenpeace's *Rainbow Warrior* was heavily involved in anti-nuclear protests, particularly against US and French nuclear testing in the Pacific Ocean, through sailing into test zones to disrupt detonations. The ship also took part in anti-whaling campaigns, confronting Soviet and Japanese whaling fleets to expose and hinder their operations. Additionally, it was used in anti-sealing protests, opposing the commercial hunting of seals, particularly in Canada, by placing activists between hunters and their prey. In the proceeding half century, extraordinary moments of civil mobilization have elevated attention onto our natural world. Most powerful to me would be 2018 to 2020, when a wave of citizens demanding climate action erupted across cities in the UK. Extinction Rebellion, with its national and local groups, began orchestrating mass marches and public occupations, calling on the government to demand a national "climate emergency". In fact, you'll find me there on the front cover of the *Guardian* coverage holding my "frack this" banner. Meanwhile, Greta Thunberg was striking school each Friday, protesting outside the Swedish parliament. Her statement was clear: why go to school when her future was in jeopardy due to climate change? Inspiring others, Greta's small action evolved into the Youth Strike for Climate movement, its effects ricocheting around the world in the early months of 2019. This so-called "youthquake" and the increased number of youth-led campaigns resulted in the announcement of the European Green New Deal, the delay of airport expansions and the halting of several new oil and gas licences.[8] On 20 September, the Global Day of Action mobilized four million people, leading to the declaration of a "climate emergency" in several countries. Simply by young people skipping school we have seen the machine of "business as usual" slow.

But I know it's not that simple and that all the above has come at a cost. I'm not talking about the cost and effort of individual habit change – recycling, consuming less, growing our own vegetables, not taking flights and a thousand other small and large acts; I'm not talking about the cost of corporate divestment in fossil fuels, switching to sustainable farming practices and electrifying our vehicles; I'm not even talking about the millions spent on research into green alternatives from biofuel to negative emissions technologies.

I'm talking here about the psychological cost. The energy drain, the burnout, the feelings of loneliness, the in-fighting, despair, grief, rage and resignation. So many young people are driven to act, to do something to help, to march, to stand up and fight, to be a part of this change-making generation, but they're stepping back from the movement as the cost of entry becomes their spirit. It's not just the climate movement, it's racial justice campaigners, gender campaigners and humanitarians. Others feel so overwhelmed by misinformation that they don't know where to begin. And a third category of us feels like for all our trying, there is no point. The surge of far right and anti-immigrant sentiment seems to have unleashed a suffocating hopelessness across borders. Danger is increasing for People of Colour, trans folk, immigrants, refugees and other historically oppressed groups. We are seeing more hostility for those seeking asylum, more protectionist policies, more anti-trans legislation and financial violence to the working class. Across all movements, we watch the scales of power tip further away from collective flourishing. Where does it leave us when we cannot give up, yet we cannot carry on?

We face an enormous number of existential challenges, with the climate and ecological emergency being the most interrelated, yet conversations about its impact on collective mental health are only just beginning. The term "eco-anxiety" is appearing in more and more news articles. Parents and adults report feeling ill-equipped to advise the younger generation about their fear, stress and uncertainty. Globally, nearly 60 per cent of young people report feeling *very* or *extremely* worried about climate change.[9] Almost 50 per cent report that their feelings about climate change negatively affect their daily life and functioning. And 75 per cent agree with the statement "the future is frightening".[10] It's also impacting our life decisions, with 48 per cent of young people in the UK and 46 per cent in the US now considering not having children. For countries like India, that figure is much higher at 75 per cent, and 64 per cent for the UEA. Burnout has become common place, now considered a key risk factor to young people taking action for the climate.[11] All of this is having an impact on mental health, which itself has become a crisis. Since the COVID-19 pandemic there has been a 25 per cent increase in depression and anxiety worldwide.[12]

The picture is complex. What I have learned from working with young people from all over the world is that this buzz word "climate anxiety" doesn't capture the full picture. It doesn't include the rage, feelings of betrayal and frustration because politicians and those in power are acknowledging the crisis on one hand, and then actively approving oil and gas fields with another. Nor does it capture the dizzying sense of urgency beyond climate, as polarization continues, genocide happens in plain sight and the refugee crisis intensifies. What I have seen consistently, from region to region, is that beyond "climate anxiety" lives loneliness. Feeling like you're the only one who cares. Feeling like it's all on you to change things. Feeling hopeless and helpless and alienated. Feeling like in vouching for kindness to people and planet, you're on the losing team.

My Story: Burnout

These feelings are familiar to me. I almost withdrew entirely from activism in my twenties. I had never conceived that climate activism or how I was doing it back then could lead to an eating disorder. Yet here I was, pinned to the bathroom floor as if the sheer weight of shame forbade me to move. I was 23, a voice in the youth climate movement, speaking on panels and at events, responsible for mobilizing thousands of young people to protest on the streets each month. I was told time and again by adults that I was awe-inspiring, a role model and I must keep going. I was told that my generation were going to "fix" this. I am thankful for these words, but the neighbour to pride is shame – and I felt shame that this supposed leader was concealing a dark secret.

I had started taking climate action with a UKYCC two years prior. We met online weekly to organize various campaigns, from attending the COP to halting fracking. It was empowering but speaking weekly about the urgency of the climate crisis led me to want to do more, and fast. A year later I established and coordinated a youth team around fossil fuels. We blockaded a fracking site for three days, joined anti-fracking mobilizations, marched with thousands of others in different UK cities, kicked-off a 500-person-strong mass-petition and hand delivered this to Westminster, where we sat in silent protest with duct tape over our mouths. Our mantra was "youth will not be silenced" and we spent a year calling out for change. While we were loud, they were quiet. The ensuing silence from government officials and corporations that followed led to splintered energy and bitter disappointment within the group. Alongside this there was in-fighting, bitching and an unspoken expectation to be the "perfect" activists. I decided to set up and hold the position of wellbeing officer, illuminating from my new vantage point what I could now see was a complex picture beyond the campaign slogans: emerging urgency, fear, burnout and depression.

Then the youth-strike movement began, whereby, inspired by Greta Thunberg, young folk started to strike school on Friday to protest government inaction. Alongside Zoe, a spirited 13-year-old, I started building the Bristol Youth Strike 4 Climate movement, which expanded from a team of 2 to 50 in the first few months. Bristol became a hub for youth climate activism, culminating with us hosting Greta Thunberg – with just five days' notice – to organize a strike event for 30,000 people. By age 23, I had led, designed and coordinated protests, marches and campaigns that mobilized over 80,000 people to demand action on climate. I became a finalist for the Global Youth Awards in 2018 in the "empowerment" category for holding a team together on banning fracking in the UK. Meanwhile I was juggling work, my studies, living with friends and the general crises of being in my early twenties. I was trying to model and guide people, some now as young as 13, through a positive, empowering and sustainable way of taking action for climate. I was trying to protect tender hearts from hopelessness and – as one of the only voices talking about wellbeing within my movements – I believed that I needed to be positive, strong and infallible at all times. My understanding of resilience at that point was that it meant being a constant support for others without collapse, holding space for everyone else's pain, fear or frustration, while at the same time somehow pretending that I was unaffected myself. It meant believing that to be strong I had to keep showing up, never waver and never admit when I was exhausted or overwhelmed. I carried the quiet expectation that I'd always be available, even when my own reserves were running dry.

I started gorging on sugary food to get quick hits of energy and keep going all day. Later I'd learn that this was known clinically as a "binge" and was a behaviour I'd repeat to provide a sense of comfort and ease during times of pressure and stress. While this was an understandable stress response, it didn't offer any self-compassion. So much of the rhetoric around climate activism orbits perfection and restriction: zero-waste, net-zero emissions, anti-plastics, no-dairy, no-meat. I imagined who the "perfect" climate activist was and how she was always energized – the embodiment of integrity – an image that became incongruent with a young woman who couldn't control herself enough to not buy stacks of plastic-clad dairy produce. I felt the pressure to be a legitimate role model for these 13-year-olds, so I developed a huge sense of shame around my binges, which in turn led to purges, which were an effective way for me to erase my mistakes. It was a vehicle for me to retain the shiny image of perfect young leader and keep up high-octane activism. It was my secret and my superpower. But I got sick very quickly.

I was working in a field where my country has left deep wounds on the world, not only by being a large contributor to global emissions since the Industrial Revolution but also a colonizer. We have caused harm through conquer and growth and I sit with all the privileges afforded to someone like me. The least responsible people – people living on the frontlines, MAPA and in the Global South – have been the most vulnerable and devastated. Convincing myself that *I* was worthy of help was a challenge, because the self-destructive coping mechanism I was choosing was nothing compared to what other people were forced to face or born into. Good solidarity became synonymous with silencing my own suffering. I told myself that I didn't have time to get help, I was making a big deal out of nothing, and I was just doing what needed to be done to execute my activism. Perspective, gratitude and empathy are crucial ingredients for solidarity, but not at the expense of your own self. Solidarity is sharing power, not bankrupting yourself in the process. In this place, nobody wins. We are all worthy of help. I know that now, but at 23 I had decided that I was going to stop climate change, and if it was at the expense of myself and my spirit, then that was a small price to pay.

Bulimia zapped me of soul and strength. I would turn up to facilitate meetings, ashen faced and with a smile painted on, because I needed to show up and be strong for everyone else. What I'd thought was my superpower was becoming my downfall, and I started to hide away from anything that wasn't climate activism. I finally told my best friend about what was happening behind closed doors, when she asked, "Where have you been? Why is your skin peeling? Why do you look so poorly?" So, I told her the truth. I had let myself be eaten alive by pressure, all the while seeing headlines that my generation were going to fix this, my generation were the beacon of hope.

My experience is not a one-off or an anomaly. In taking on the challenge of the ages, many of us – but particularly young people – are encountering a new form of pressure, uncertainty and burden that other generations may not have known. I have worked with young people, some identifying as "activists" and others who simply want to have a say in their own future, and they have confided in me feelings ranging from guilt over plastic use to suicidal ideation. They themselves and their friends are being arrested, they feel the intergenerational rift, they are tokenised, youthwashed and ignored.* Their subconscious minds are flooded with the existential risk to life that is here and is not slowing down. It's an oversimplification to reduce this to "climate anxiety."

It's Not Just Me

The climate activist you are following on social media will have been sick this year. They will have shared that they are feeling exhausted and tired, and that they keep crying. They might use the phrase "burnout". This same person, in different seasons, will talk about the fundamental importance of rest, joy and community, describing these as preventative measures to burnout. Yet the cycles of boom and bust, where we feel strong and then feel meek, seem to relentlessly continue. This person is me and maybe you.

I barely know anyone in the youth movement, particularly who came up through the 2019 youthquake, who hasn't experienced some kind of burnout and taken a significant chunk of time off. I've also heard this from people not in the youth movement. I've heard it from investment bankers, aid workers and actors. Exhaustion seems to be seeping into my generation. Why? I've flirted with the idea that the term has become mainstream and consequently incorrectly used. In fact, I spoke with a psychologist on the matter, who shared her frustrations that young people were co-opting the phrase. Burnout, in her understanding, is something that occurs

* Youthwashing (similar to greenwashing) was first brought to my attention by Scottish climate campaigner Eilidh Robb. She describes it as the use of youth-centred marketing, imagery, language and endorsements to try to improve the public image of a company, policy or activity. This practice sprang up significantly in the aftermath of the youth climate strike movement in 2020 and was used by fossil fuel companies to try to broaden their public appeal.

when an adult moves through similar behaviour patterns without adjustment, leading to cycles of the same outcomes and ultimately breakdown. Due to the cyclical nature of burnout, she suggested that young people can't be burned out, as they haven't been living long enough. Another burnout dismissal I've heard is that my generation are snowflakes, confusing tiredness with exhaustion and stress with burnout. With all due respect for the discipline of psychology, in my own work I have largely dismissed both these suggestions as I feel that neither grapple with what I am actually seeing. The volume of symptoms I see around me goes far beyond "I'm tired". I have heard testimonials of suicidal ideation, apathy, resignation and a handful of friends have been hospitalized due to the knock-on effects of stress. "Chronic fatigue" and diagnoses of meningitis have been more frequent, and I'm not chalking this up to coincidence.

These mental health impacts have different names and diagnoses, but they all speak to our relationship with stress, responsibility, social relations, visibility and burden. While my enquiry began with my own burnout in 2019, I didn't begin to use that language until afterwards. Officially, I had developed an eating disorder. But underneath, I had developed a strategy to cope with the stress of changemaking and the constant visibility of being a so-called leader. Burnout therefore became helpful language to begin making sense of why I was struggling to regulate myself emotionally, why I felt a dullness around my life and why I felt lost. You'll hear me refer to that time as "something which *felt* like burnout", because we can debate terminology all day long, but we can't debate our feelings and experiences. The rational mind can busy itself over language and semantics, but the body is the true litmus test for our experience. We get sick. Our digestive system gives us trouble. We can't sleep. Our bodies carry the wisdom our minds forbid us to know. More on that in Chapter 9 and in Tori Tsui's book *It's Not Just You.*[13]

Burnout Prevention: Visibility and Stress

"Why are the kids all depressed? Social media!" I hear in news soundbites. It's banal to equate burnout and social media. As with all tools, it's how you use them. Where I see exhaustion arising is less about social media itself and more about how it gives the user the impression of constantly visibility. There has been no other time in human history when people have been reachable, cross-continent, 24 hours a day, 7 days a week. As mortal beings, expecting ourselves to be ever available and indefinitely productive is a high bar to set. Cars need fuelling, trees shed their leaves and even phones need updates. With the possible exception of the sun, we have few examples of how always being "on" is conducive to thriving. No wonder we are all feeling so exhausted.

To explain my point, let's look to the work of philosopher Michel Foucault and his concept of the *Panopticon*.[14] His theory was based on Jeremy Bentham's architectural design for prisons. The Panopticon is a circular prison building with a central watchtower. The guard sits in the middle watchtower with darkened windows, obscured from view, and the inmates are housed in cells around the tower against the circular wall.

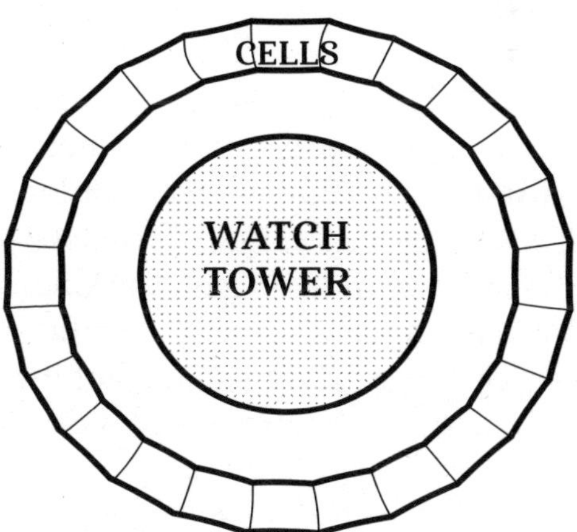

Figure 1: A diagram of the Panopticon prison design, with a central guard in the middle watch tower, and inmates cells on the sides, facing inward. [15]

This circular design leave inmates unsure if or when they are being watched. In theory, this uncertainty creates self-regulating good behaviour among the inmates: because they are unsure of when or whether they're being watched, they comply all the time. The idea runs that inmates will internalize the gaze of authority and begin "self-policing" their behaviour. Hence, regardless of whether authority is in the watchtower or not, good behaviour and self-policing continue. Foucault uses this metaphor to illustrate how modern society disciplines and conditions behaviour through constant surveillance, leading people to internalize norms and regulate their own behaviour.

Social media can be seen as a *digital* Panopticon, an omnipresent watchtower where users are perpetually observed, not by a single authority figure, but by peers, algorithms and the broader public. Gen-Z and late millennials, who have largely grown up immersed in digital culture, are subject to this ever-present visibility causing their own form of self-discipline. Likes, shares and comments serve as forms of approval, reinforcing behaviour and creating pressure to maintain a visible stance on issues. Constant visibility and fear of judgement can contribute to us feeling compelled to consistently perform our values online, even at the cost of mental anguish. At our Residentials I've heard from youth speaking about this candidly. They've shared about the pressure they feel, not from one individual, but from the elusive collective (the watchtower) to constantly post about the latest injustice, react to current events or demonstrate their commitment, even if they're not fully educated about it. This "always-on" nature of social media leaves little room for rest, reflection or nuance and importantly it distracts from the very real and genuine material work on solidarity and justice.

You might identify with the familiar feeling of posting something online, either about the world or just your weekend or how you are feeling. Against all our wisest internal counsels, we range from mildly interested to obsessed with its level of engagement. We find ourselves picking up our phone more to see how it's doing, who has liked it or, importantly, who hasn't. Or perhaps we've shared or posted something and immediately deleted it, for fear of disapproval by the omnipresent watchtower. *Maybe it was too cringe? Not well-informed enough? Does anybody care? Am I coming across as a vibe-kill?* Self-doubt feels ever present. This constant need to prove our engagement and values can mirror the self-regulating behaviour described by Foucault, where individuals internalize the expectations and surveillance of their peers.

Digital activism is a complex topic and I don't have all the answers. Sharing online is fundamental for amplifying struggles and messages. For those with a platform, there is a sense of moral duty to uplift other voices. In the same breath, positive change happened before social media and digital activism isn't the only modality for engagement. While I lack answers, I notice observations that feel important to air in the context of resilience. The expectation to continuously engage, educate others and respond to ever-evolving crises places a heavy emotional and cognitive load on young people. Our posting or not posting may have very little or even nothing to do with what campaigns we are working on, how we are spending charitable money and what makes us cry in private. In such a highly visible space, there can be a fine line between genuine advocacy and performative activism, posting not out of authentic commitment but out of fear of judgement or the desire for approval. Unlike the prisoners in Foucault's model, who are watched by a central authority, social media users are subject to a decentralized and potentially limitless gaze. This hypervisibility increases the risk of harassment, trolling and public shaming, which further exacerbates stress and can lead to withdrawal.

How do we overcome the burden of visibility? Firstly, it's important to consider the role each of us plays in the watchtower itself. Are we complicit in judgement and shame? Do we judge someone's worth as a changemaker by how much they engage online? As an individual, it's a moral imperative for our movement to unpick when you're posting to drive change and when you are virtue signalling. What can help here is cultivating boundaries – for example, choosing when to engage and being selective with sharing, rather than rapidly reacting. Digital detoxes are also becoming more common, as are self-timer limit apps on social media. Ultimately, billions of dollars have been spent on capturing your attention and locking you into social media use. A great first step is an awareness of the Panopticon and how visibility and burden carry a cognitive load.

Looking Back and Moving Forward

If I could go back in time and talk to my 23-year-old self, sitting with stress-induced bulimia, I would tell her that this battle should never have been hers to fight alone. Climate action is essential and empowering, but it's also such a large, widespread and complex challenge that it requires a deep personal inventory of support tools and strong structures of peer support before, during and after. We need every person involved, but not all the time and not giving all of themselves. This is a team sport.

During what felt like a crisis moment, I resolved to get help. I started my recovery journey and stepped back from activism. I took some time to reflect on my experience of being young and passionate about the future. Is the methodology of change really millions of young people taking action and then feeling wiped out by burnout or resignation in six months' time? Does change need to come at the expense of the mental health of a generation? Is that something I want to be an advocate for? I knew that as a collective we needed to keep going – we were a powerful force, but our energy was finite. So instead of quitting, I rested. I took myself away, sat and thought and thought and thought. What emerged was a realization that we needed not just funding or numbers or a new strategy, we needed each other. The solidarity, care and support we extend to ourselves and one another aren't luxuries, but the essential foundations of all we hope to build. While collective wellbeing alone won't save the planet, it is what strengthens the people who will.

In 2020, a year later, while the world was moving through tremendous change, I set up The Resilience Project to do right by 23-year-old Katie, to be the support that she had been crying out for. I wanted to ensure that those courageously stepping up for the planet would be rewarded with joy, community and personal growth rather than burnout, climate anxiety and despair. It sent me on a journey to breathe life into an organization that radically challenges how we are doing things. It is by youth, for youth and we've now worked with thousands of youths.

CHAPTER 3: "INNER-TERSECTIONAL" CHANGEMAKING

Sustainable changemaking demands more than external action, it requires profound internal transformation too. "Inner development", far from New Age spirituality, is becoming a globally recognized field. For example, The Inner Development Goals (IDGs) initiative suggests that we haven't met the Sustainable Development Goals because we have under resourced the interpersonal skills required to make such change. The IDGs isolate the five key "inner" skills required: being, collaborating, action, thinking and relating. Each dimension contains sub-skills – for example, "collaborating" includes communication skills, co-creation skills, inclusive mindset, intercultural competence, trust and mobilization skills. Thinking includes critical thinking, complexity awareness, perspective skills, sense-making and long-term orientation and visioning. This takes "inner work" far beyond meditation and journalling and is concerned more with how we build solidarity across movements with sensitivity, as well as how we develop and foster trust within ourselves and others.

Inner work is a necessary condition for world shift, but it is not sufficient on its own. The addendum is significant. When I was 20 years old, I spent one month in a meditation community where people existed off-grid, so engrossed in their internal landscape that conversations of social injustice blew past them like leaves. The central idea of this kind of meditation, someone once explained to me, was that focusing on our own internal work will make a generation of conscious agents. But the idea that spiritual practice alone will transform eight billion people both ignores enormous systemic barriers and is working to a timescale that we simply don't have. Secondly, a spirituality which foregrounds *personal* prosperity rather than collective, to me, doesn't capture what is at the heart of spiritual endeavour: to decentre the ego enough to appreciate that we are all equal (in our humanity) and all deserving of justice and peace. Therefore, a spirituality without social justice misses the point. At age 20, meditating in that community in the mountains, while not looking at the world, I found stillness, happiness and joy. But resilience is forged not by how calmly we can sit in the shadows, but how tall we stand in the wicked winds. That happiness grew out of shielding my eyes from suffering and therefore it was eviscerated once I left the sanctuary. As I posited in the introduction, though I had found wellness, stepping out into the real world and then losing it felt like a personal failure.

The Macro: Systems Change and Intersectionality

I would argue that we need inner work but not just inner work. Because *attitude* doesn't equal *action*. Attitude without practice is performative. Then a second concept I introduce is "intersectionality", illuminating how we understand society and power. Intersectionality is a framework for understanding how various forms of social identities – such as race, gender, class, sexuality, disability, and more – intersect and overlap, creating complex layers of discrimination and privilege. The concept was first coined by Kimberlé Crenshaw in 1989, though its roots can be traced back to Black feminist thought

Attitude doesn't equal *action*. Attitude without practice is performative.

and the work of activists such as Sojourner Truth. Crenshaw introduced the term in her paper "Demarginalizing the Intersection of Race and Sex", where she analysed how Black women face unique challenges due to the combined effects of racism and sexism. Her work demonstrated that social justice frameworks often failed to address the compounded nature of oppression experienced by individuals who occupy multiple marginalized identities.

Historically, feminist and anti-racist movements have sometimes overlooked the specific needs of those who exist at the intersections of various identities. For example, the mainstream feminist movement often centred the experiences of white, middle-class women, while anti-racist movements, in some cases, focused primarily on the struggles of Black men. Crenshaw's intersectionality theory sought to challenge this single-axis analysis by demonstrating how Black women experience both gender and racial discrimination in ways that are not simply additive but interlocking and complex.

Intersectionality as a lens has been applied in fields ranging from sociology to law to public policy. For example, in legal contexts, intersectionality is used to highlight how discrimination laws, which tend to treat race, gender or other categories as separate issues, may fail to address the full scope of discrimination that people with intersecting identities face.

Intersectional environmentalism is an extension of this concept. Coined by US youth environmental activist Leah Thomas during the rise of the Black Lives Matter movement, intersectional environmentalism highlights the connections between environmental degradation and social injustice.[16] Leah brought this concept to the forefront by emphasizing that environmental justice cannot be separated from racial and social justice – just as intersectionality examines overlapping forms of oppression, intersectional environmentalism calls for a more inclusive approach to environmentalism by connecting the dots between individual issues and the system. It gives rise to the common notion in the youth climate movement that there is no climate justice without racial justice, gender justice, class justice, disability justice and more, because climate breakdown and climate injustice are inherently linked to wider systems of capitalism, colonialism, patriarchy and white supremacy.

To ground this further, here are a few examples.

1. Climate justice equals racial justice. Low-income and predominantly Black, Indigenous and People of Colour (BIPOC) families and communities are more likely to live near polluting industries, motorways, landfills and toxic waste sites. They have been disadvantaged not by personal circumstance, but by colonialism, land-grabbing and systemic racism. These households and communities often face greater exposure to harmful environmental conditions, such as contaminated water, air pollution and the impacts of climate change while having fewer resources to protect themselves or recover from environmental disasters.
2. Climate justice equals gender justice. Globally, women bear the burden of the climate crisis. They generally have less access to land ownership, financial resources and political power, meaning that they are more vulnerable to climate-related displacement and poverty. Their traditional role in care and household roles means that they have more responsibility for securing resources like water, food and fuel for their households. As droughts, floods and other environmental disasters worsen, these resources become scarcer, increasing the burden on women, who may have to travel longer distances or face unsafe conditions to find them.
3. Climate justice equals disability justice. During extreme weather events like hurricanes, heatwaves or wildfires, individuals with disabilities often face additional challenges, such as lack of accessible evacuation routes, shelters not being equipped to meet their needs or limited access to

critical medical supplies. This became a reality during Hurricane Katrina in the USA in 2005, when many disabled people were left behind due to inaccessible transportation and insufficient emergency planning.

4. Climate justice equals migrant justice. It is estimated that 216 million individuals may be forced to migrate within their own countries across six world regions due to climate-related factors such as water scarcity, crop failure and sea-level rise.[17] Additionally, the Institute for Economics and Peace predicts that an enormous 1.2 billion people could be displaced globally by 2050 due to extreme weather and natural disasters.[18] These climate-induced displacements often intersect with existing inequalities shaped by colonial histories and uneven development. In this view, advocating for climate justice inherently includes fighting for the rights, dignity and protection of migrants, refugees and those seeking asylum uprooted by ecological collapse.

These short examples are by no means exhaustive, yet they uncover the complex and intersecting threads of identity and discrimination. Traditional environmental movements have often been critiqued for focusing on conservation, wildlife and nature preservation while ignoring or underemphasizing the social injustices tied to environmental issues. By embracing intersectionality, movements and campaigns strive for a more inclusive approach, which acknowledges the different ways people are impacted by systemic oppression. Intersectionality focuses not just on single issues like recycling but also on dismantling the systemic racism, classism and other forms of inequality that amplify environmental harm for certain groups. An intersectional approach to climate solutions could look like green jobs and clean energy in low-income areas, Indigenous land and water rights and addressing the disproportionate impacts of climate change on MAPA groups. In essence, if single-issue environmentalism is treating a symptom, intersectional approaches attempt to treat the disease – the disease being unfair and unequal systems that safeguard the status-quo. Leah Thomas's Intersectional Environmentalist platform and book, as well as similar movements, work to educate people on the importance of understanding the environment through a wider lens. Inclusive policies should not only fight ecological degradation but also ensure that marginalized communities are at the forefront of decision-making processes.

Toward "Inner-tersectionality"

This is big stuff, right? A lot more than doing our bit by having shorter showers. In moving from single-issue campaigning to intersectional, we are requiring individuals and groups to hold a much wider view. Take, for example, electric cars. Single-issue campaigning might call for a switch from petrol to electric cars, whereas intersectional campaigning considers that meeting the rising demand for electric cars in affluent households in the Global North requires the mining of the minerals and lithium for batteries, which incurs human rights violations and utilizes child labour in some parts of the Democratic Republic of Congo. An intersectional environmentalist might pull together the threads of capitalism and colonialism and opt for lower consumption as the solution rather than electric vehicles, or campaign for additional legislation to protect workers in kind. This is not to dampen the spirits of anyone advocating for electrifying. Intersectionality simply invites a wider gaze at the historic currents of power and how these continue to play out through our contemporary actions. The common cry for "system change, not climate change" involves looking very deeply at systems that perpetuate harm. Intersectional campaigning invites us to assess our own levels of power and then to redistribute it to those historically afforded less. How much "power" and "access" we respectively have is more nuanced than just race, gender, ability, class and sexuality. It also includes our lineage, upbringing, follower count, body shape and how conventionally attractive we are.

We are right to ask more from our campaigns and our movements. What I'm trying to get at is that asking young people to grapple with enormous, global challenges requires more than tactics and training; it demands resilience, self-awareness and a holistic vision of change. To hold bigger challenges, we need to be better resourced. That means our movements and changemakers need to be financially equipped and trained but also rooted in collective resilience, humility to listen and self-awareness.

It is the interweaving of three powerful frameworks: intersectionality, intersectional environmentalism and inner development that I call "*inner*-tersectional changemaking". This holistic approach to changemaking integrates inner development with collective justice, recognizing that lasting change requires both inner transformation and systemic disruption. It includes holding both the complex systems of the world and the complex selves that we are; it's a call to action and to introspection. It also emphasizes that true transformation arises from integrating the macro – societal systems of power and injustice – with the micro – the inner landscapes of our minds and behaviours. A more active approach to "be the change you want to see in the world", innertersectional changemaking acknowledges the dual responsibility of inward growth and outward action.

Just engaging with inner work might leave us too passive as we see too little. Just engaging with intersectional work might leave us too activated as we see too much. One of the core principles of innertersectional changemaking is the idea that inner and outer change are in fact mutually re-enforcing. When we cultivate inner resilience, we become more effective at challenging oppressive systems. When we engage in intersectional changemaking, we deepen our understanding of ourselves and our position in the world. The two are inextricably linked, each strengthening and informing the other. Consider the activist who campaigns tirelessly for climate justice, but their imposter syndrome stops them from speaking up effectively. Or the social justice advocate who is deeply committed to equity but their overidentification with work is leading to burnout. Innertersectional changemaking calls us to honour these inner battles, not as separate from the fight for systemic change but as integral to it. Inner and outer transformation are inseparable.

The journey of inner development is deeply personal, but it also has profound implications for collective change. Looking at our inner saboteurs can transform our ability to persevere through setbacks. Learning to navigate our own fear and anxiety makes us better equipped to hold space for others. When we practise empathy and self-awareness, we become more effective allies and coalition-builders. Inner development strengthens our capacity to stand in solidarity with others, even when the road is long and challenging.

Innertersectional Solutions

In my own changemaking journey, I have lost interest in a "climate solution" that doesn't consider both the systemic and inner-led components to change. Advances in climate technology might suck trillions of CO_2 particles out of the air, yes, but then what are we left with? We still have a failing system where suicide is one of the biggest killers for young men in the UK under the age of 35; where greed causes civilian causalities in gut-wrenching numbers; and where unequal gender relations cause women to live with preconceived limitations. We still sit in a polarized world where cancel culture feels easier than engaging in uncomfortable conversations. We still have political factions where fixation on our identity can keep us in echo chambers and deny many of us (with the safety to do so) of learning and understanding. We are still afflicted by the degradation of the soul.

Innertersectional changemaking means bringing human nature to the foreground. It requires not only mobilizing against those who vote for harm but also practising enough compassion so as not to recreate the "us", "them" and "the other" dynamic. It asks us to momentarily pause our obsession with the out-there and take a long hard look at our justice movements too and systems of harm we may be perpetuating internally. For example, I see great changemakers and movements, but I still see ego, career-hunger, vanity, cliques, jealousy and tearing each other down when we don't meet the unrealistic standards we ask of one another. I see people dismissing others if their chosen career path is not presently world-changing, rather than seeing the complexities that sit inside them, such as financial insecurity or a lack of mentorship to walk a different path. They only see their complicity in the "system". This isn't the same as giving people permission to be shit. It's to engage actively with the judgements in our mind, the assumptions and the discomfort, rather than to turn away and question if this helps or hinders us (the micro) and the wider movement (the macro). The notion "if you think this, we are no longer friends" is common on my timeline, without an appreciation that the person you dismiss has an invisible history of personal circumstances, familial relationships and, perhaps, pain. It erodes their humanity and their innate ability to change their mind. The "inner" invites more compassion, empathy and understanding. It's not easy work but it's essential if we want to better ourselves, our planet and our collective psyche.

CHAPTER 4:
INTERNAL ACTIVATION FOR EXTERNAL ACTION

When I first became captivated by the climate crisis, I found a different kind of fear. It wasn't just the fear of planetary collapse or extreme weather. No, it was the fear of being exposed, of being labelled a fraud. I was consumed by imposter syndrome. I was hesitant to step into the youth climate space because I lacked a deep understanding of climate science, geography or environmental policy. I felt that my voice didn't matter and had little to contribute. I wasn't an "activist" in the way others at my university were – I didn't know what Net Zero really meant or how to make homemade kimchi. The idea that I wasn't knowledgeable enough kept me from joining a movement. When I eventually did, I was armed with my camera, to convince myself that videography was how I could meaningfully contribute. I still constantly feared being grilled by a journalist with hard-hitting questions or being challenged at family gatherings on green politics. When I heard others in my campaign group talking eloquently and knowledgeably about politics or theories, I didn't see them for the miracle that they are, selflessly giving up their time for service, I saw them through the eyes of jealousy, competition and my own inadequacy.

Imposter syndrome remains one of the most common internal hinderances to creating external impact. While it

may seem trivial against the backdrop of a global crisis, it's a deeply human and widespread response, transcending age and borders. Imposter syndrome hinders us in several ways. If you constantly feel like you're not "qualified enough" or "not doing enough", you're less likely to speak up, lead initiatives or contribute ideas, especially in activist spaces that can already feel intense or competitive. It drives us to overwork to prove we're good enough. In changemaking, this often means taking on too much, ignoring your boundaries or tying your worth to your output. Finally, it makes perfection the enemy of progress. There may be a fear of getting things wrong, particularly around privilege, language and identity, which results in a hesitancy to speak up and letting mistakes feel like identity threats. You might fear being found to be not as virtuous or well-educated or inclusive as you'd like. All of these things stifle the gifts we possess to contribute.

How to Overcome Imposter Syndrome

Imposter syndrome gives the illusion that there are entry requirements to becoming a "valid" enough changemaker. What is your benchmark for being a legitimate changemaker? Perhaps it's an understanding of climate systems or full working knowledge of degrowth environmentalism. Perhaps it's having the term "activist" in your Instagram bio or getting arrested in direct action. Perhaps it's a mullet (not a requirement but definitely a bonus).

Overcoming imposter syndrome requires recognizing that there is only one requirement to being a legitimate changemaker: the courage to care. Access to knowledge and information divides us, often employed intentionally by climate sceptics to sow doubt in the climate agenda. Facts and figures have become ammunition in ideological battles. But the simple act of caring cannot be falsified. Caring can't be disputed. What makes you a legitimate voice in your school's newsletter? What validates you voting green? What makes you enough by sharing your thoughts on social media? The answer is *you care about life beyond yourself.*

Caring is not the comfortable option. That's why it requires courage.

It's easy to feel that those of us who hope for a better future are in the minority. Caring is not the comfortable option. That's why it requires courage. You will meet discomfort time and time again. Firstly, confronting the reality of our crises is profoundly unsettling and we've become unaccustomed to truly facing our anxieties. Netflix, social media, Uber, Google Maps and the gig-economy are reminders that there is a huge market for comfort and wellness hacks. Secondly, many crises we face are not the product of chance encounters, but the result of decisions made by powerful people. For example, climate breakdown has seen millions of dollars funnelled into climate denial and climate scepticism in the US since the 1980s. A small collection of wealthy Western men peddled denial because climate action and systems change threatened their business interests and the Republican status quo.[19] Yikes. It takes courage to consider mobilizing against such powerful and covert factions and sit in the discomfort that you might lose. Thirdly, climate breakdown highlights how inequality and injustice have shaped our world and continue to do so. If you're reading this as a person from the Global North, particularly the UK or US, then it requires courage to sit in the discomfort of the extreme *relative* privilege we have. If you're reading this as a white Eurocentric person, engaging with climate will lead you to your ancestors' history of colonialism and Western imperialism, which has actively harmed so many for the benefit of the few. Being confronted with the reality that you may benefit from historic systems that disadvantage others, even unintentionally, is uncomfortable as it feels like it invalidates one as a "good" person. Meaningful climate justice involves unpacking "whiteness" and how white supremacy leaves its traces not only on resource allocation but on our aspirations and unconscious biases. Allyship is uncomfortable because it involves stepping back so others can lead, which can feel threatening in a culture that prizes control, visibility and authority. Fourthly, being part of a group calling for things to be different will require what some perceive as "radical" behaviour and decisions. It requires the courage to walk the road less travelled, from asking your family for vegan options at Christmas to boycotting certain events your friends are attending. To stand for something is often to stand alone.

Choosing a life of courage over comfort is not easy, but it's necessary. For the world, for future generations, and for our own growth and actualization. It means confronting loneliness, uncertainty and the quiet inner voices that tell us we're not good enough or a killjoy. There are no shortcuts to transforming the world or ourselves – no hacks. Both require depth, discomfort and a willingness to stay with what feels hard. Another reminder of why innertersectional changemaking is so crucial moving forward.

Choosing a life of courage over comfort is not easy, but it's necessary.

The easiest way to overcome imposter syndrome? Retreat. Disengage. Shrink yourself until the risk disappears. Stop showing up. It's an alluring option, because hiding offers instant relief. But where is the life in that? Where is the connection, the expansion, the learning? Retreat, in this sense, becomes the deadening of our response. It's the quiet reinforcement of the belief that we do not belong, and worse, that we never did. The real work lies not in perfecting ourselves before we participate, but in choosing to show up as we are: authenticity. It lies in taking up space even while your voice trembles. It's in being tender with yourself when the doubt sets in, and still saying: I am here, and I matter. Grace, not grit, is what we need most in these moments. Grace to try, to get it wrong, to learn out loud and to stay in the room anyway. In the hall of world-shakers and move-makers, you have your place because you care. Now that's some powerful internal activation.

External activism is the work of altering systems, structures, culture and policies. It includes campaigns, policy advocacy, community organizing, mutual aid, direct action, discourse analysis, art and more. Internal activation is the journey of consistently switching on to the fact again and again that you aren't just changing systems and structures but are part of them, moulded by them. You have inherited beliefs, narratives, emotional patterns and ways of relating to yourself, which may even mirror the injustices we seek to change in the world. Internal activation is the deliberate process of transforming and tending to your inner landscape so you can show up in the world with greater clarity, resilience and integrity. Importantly, it begins to dissolve the boundary between you as a person and your identity as an activist. For example, internal activation may illuminate patterns of "not-enoughness" you may have learned as a child, which you carry into your changemaking settings. Hence, anything internal observation which arises through external activism will likely be a pattern you express in your personal life. Taking action without burning out requires balancing our internal activation with our external activism. Internal activation is the inhale, the drawing in; external action is the exhale, the offering out. That's how we sustain life.

> Internal activation is the inhale, external action is the exhale.

Stepping into the Arena

What has aided me on my enquiry into internal activation has been the idea of the Arena: the Colosseum in Rome. Paul Mescal. You get the drift. It's an imaginary *Gladiator*-esque set-up in my mind of captor versus foe, voracious applause and dramatic sequences. To look at the world and think "that's not right and I want to do something about it" is to step into the Arena. It's a place that the courageous step into when they decide to stand against the oppressor. In true *Gladiator* style, this would usually be citizen or an enslaved person against a trained soldier, which mirrors the power asymmetry exhibited in changemaking.

Historically, striving for change has placed grassroots and marginalized groups against a well-funded, well-connected and well-organized opponent. Take LGBTQ+ activists. They have stood – and still stand – against historic religious tenants and teachings that invalidate their existence, alongside an ideological battle driven by right-wing political factions. Or Indigenous peoples, who are having their land grabbed and seized by giant corporations for production, who are armed with legal expertise and the money to match. To step into the Arena is to knowingly stand in a space against power. To be on the side of change rather than the status quo is to be the whistle-blower, the dissident voice and the compassionate agitator. This means you begin on the back foot. Stepping into the Arena requires an understanding that, guess what, you're going to get your butt kicked. I need that to sink in: getting your butted kicked is an inevitability – but it's not the whole story.

In countries like Columbia, Brazil, Mexico and Honduras, stepping into the Arena can be a life-or-death decision. Between 2012 and 2022, almost 2,000 environmental defenders have been killed, with their families never receiving justice. In 2022, the killing rate equated to one defender death every other day. I often feel the weight of exhaustion as I step into the Arena, but it's a privilege to do so without fear of extreme physical harm. We owe a debt of gratitude to those environmental defenders whose lives have been taken and those who continue to fight in such countries for truth and change. You can read their names through the Global Witness database and honour their legacy by connecting the dots between our struggles.[20]

For many like me, our proximity to persecution has been intensifying in the last few years. The Public Order Act 2023 introduced stricter laws targeting protest tactics in England and Wales, including criminalizing the "locking on" tactic and allowing stop-and-search powers without suspicion. Prison sentences for activists have become longer, including an eye-watering three-year sentence for two climate activists who scaled a bridge and displayed a movement flag. Though we rarely risk threat to life, entering the Arena comes with an increasing psychological toll. Because to bring "change" is to disturb giant structures of historic power, centuries of stories being understood as "truths" and active and covert campaigns backed by millions of dollars to continue "business-as-usual".

Burnout Is an Occupational Hazard

This might be the most pertinent point of this book, so buckle up. To stand in the Arena is to accept that you will move in consistent *proximity* to burnout. Changemaking is extraordinarily hard, especially if you possess an identity devalued by society, or you have fewer resources or you work across multiple fronts of changemaking. Activism will leave you in constant proximity to burnout because there is no version of upheaving systems, facing consistent losses or feeling on the margins that does not involve challenge. This acceptance that burnout is built into the fabric of the Arena is not acceptance of that as a fate. It provides a balm to feelings of exhaustion because of course you are feeling tired, this work is tough. Of course you keep crying for no reason, you are stepping into a space of death, grief and anguish. Of course you're exhausted, you're a 22-year-old up against an oil and gas lobby valued at $4.3 trillion. Of course you're fatigued, capitalism has devalued rest and the rent is due. Step one is an acceptance that in courageously calling for a different paradigm, the processes of creating, melting and making requires heat. You might get burned.

My framing should not be equated to defeatism. Changemaking is not a one-way street to burnout, but an invitation to understand our needs and requirements for sustained strength. In knowing and accepting that the forge of change carries heat, we can adapt and sharpen our mind, behaviours and armour. As mentioned, the definition of resilience is not the absence of storms, it is how we move through them, how we bounce back. In the case of changemaking, it is not building a life that avoids stress and tiredness and loss. If that were the case, you wouldn't be reading this book. It's about building a life where our relationship with stress and tiredness also creates space for aliveness. One part of me feels deeply tired, yes, but how can other parts of me feel alive?

To be in the Arena is not to be defeated. It's to lose and win and win and win and lose again and again. You don't need to throw in the towel and leave the Arena – you're in the bravest, most courageous and exciting place – a place where heroes are born and odds are overturned. What you need is the resilience to get back up and go again, and a team to support and hold you. It's about finding the person, or people, who don't say, "You're fighting a losing battle – what's the point?" but rather, "What do you need to get back in or go again?" With support and love, we learn to rest, reset and repeat, not to quit.

With support and love, we learn to rest, reset and repeat, not to quit.

The metaphor of the Arena provides therapeutic value to me as it places my exhaustion in the realms of the rational. How would you imagine yourself in a battle stadium facing a powerful foe? You'd be exhausted. So, stepping up for change may result in the same feelings. Re-understanding these emotions as "rational" might not get rid of them entirely, but it can ease additional feelings of shame or surprise, as the question "but why do I feel like this?!" is partially answered. What requires some thinking then is how we armour ourselves while here. This means considering how to build resilience'. How can we feel better equipped for vulnerability and failure?

You Are Going to Feel

Since burnout, the Arena has changed in my mind. No longer do I stand alone. The burden of the struggle is not just mine to hold. Now I see the soft sand of the Arena as my community, cushioning any falls. The stadium is filled with my ancestors, the movers and shakers who have courageously laid the groundwork for change, and those yet to come who will thank me for being courageous enough to try. My movement, ones who I know and ones who I don't, are on the bench ready to be tapped in at any time.

To me, to be in the Arena is to *feel*. You're going to feel pain and fear, triumph and glory, pride and shame. And perhaps that's why many refrain from stepping inside, because the Arena points floodlights at some of our most uncomfortable emotions. It illuminates the human vulnerability that we might sometimes lose. But it is also a place of hope. As playwright Václav Havel stated: "Hope is not the conviction that something will turn out well but the certainty that something is worth doing no matter how it turns out."[21]

Stepping into the Arena, though grand in its imagery, happens in both large and very small ways. Not everyone has the time and resources to affect change in big ways, and nobody should be expecting people to give up job security to become a full-time volunteer. But in the small, there is *always* choice. A quote I hold close comes from Viktor Frankl's famous *Man's Search for Meaning*, where he details that even though everything you possess can be taken from you at any given moment, you still have "your freedom to choose how you will respond to the situation".[22] Striking up a conversation with someone who looks lost and lonely requires courage as they might reject our invitation, yet it might make their day or impact them profoundly in ways that we'll never be able to foresee. This kind of changemaking, though seemingly small, directly resists the neoliberal ideas of "individualism" and the Age of Loneliness. When you apologize to someone for your wrongdoings, you expose yourself to the vulnerability of rejection, but you also call into practice a world of retribution, accountability and growth.

While these examples might not feel directly relevant to changemaking, I argue that they are. Because the more we express courage for the sake of kindness, compassion and connection, the nearer we move to the kind of world we are calling in. Not only do we resist the narratives that cause harm, such as individualism, scarcity and greed, but expressing courage is a muscle we strengthen. Courage is cumulative. When we engage in small acts, we expose ourselves to the practice required for larger courageous acts. Like cash in the bank, small acts contribute to our overall resources of courage, which may be required to make a big speech, pitch a campaign idea or call out hate speech. You might find that the more you practise it in your personal life, the easier you might find it to engage with a climate sceptic or post your thoughts and feelings about greenwashing online. In both the big and small ways, step into the Arena – I'll be in the stands, cheering you on.

PART TWO

CHAPTER 5:

GUIDEPOST 1 – HUMANS FIRST, CHANGEMAKERS SECOND

"If I can't dance, it's not my revolution."[23]

Emma Goldman

It was 2020, a year characterized by turbulence, burnout and isolation, and the power of the youth climate movement was beginning to wane. I knew I wanted to take action to fight the rising insurgency of fatigue, but I lacked the confidence. Only when an older activist, Bethan Harris, said she'd support me did I realize it would be foolish not to try. She offered her organization as the fiscal host for my project, meaning that I could access funding. After securing a tiny pot of seed funding, I started to build what would become The Resilience Project.

The work demanded a dozen hats: fundraiser, programme designer and reluctant communications expert. One afternoon, while I was talking it through with my friend Mick, he said, "Katie, I'm curious. How will you *amplify* the message of resilient campaigning if you've got about six followers on social media?" Always a straight shooter, our Mick.

He pushed on. "Listen, I've got time during my lunch breaks. Give me your login and I'll follow the accounts you want to engage. Politically engaged young people, right?" It was an offer I jumped at. Support with social media would free me up to keep deep diving into why so many of us were so burned out. Little did I know that he'd be finding part of the answer. I handed over my password, thanked him and went back to my spreadsheets.

We met a few weeks later for a coffee. "So," he announced, sliding into the booth, "I've followed and gained about a thousand people for you. You owe me five coffees, minimum – and probably a wage."

I was elated. One thousand followers in two weeks. I'd been watching the number creep up. Engagement was steady and the initiative suddenly felt real. Curious to know his secret, I asked how he'd managed it so quickly.

"Easy." He said, "All the youth activists – including you – have the same bio on Instagram. They state their name, age, pronouns, insert emoji of choice and then it states anti-climate change, trans rights, anti-capitalist, anti-insert-'ism' and final emoji to cushion the sentiment. I click follow. They follow back. They comment on how much something like this is needed. Voilà."

I took a look through our followers and found that he was spot on. So many accounts defined themself by what they were for or against in the changemaking space. It was a nuanced bit of psychosocial insight that I couldn't shake for years: the tension between defining (or presenting) ourselves by important values, but not reducing ourselves down to a changemaker first, human second. Was this my truth too? Did I define myself by what I was against rather than what I was fighting for? Absolutely.

As changemakers or activists or simply those who wish for a fairer world, it is easy to become deeply enmeshed with our work. There is immense power, requirement and pride in having this clarity of purpose, but when changemaking becomes the singular lens through which we view ourselves, it can also bring challenges. Over-identifying with the label of "activist" or "changemaker" can cause more harm than good. It can lead to moral battlegrounds and alienation from those closest to us, creating barriers in conversations with family and friends who may not share or understand our perspectives. It can also distort our work–life balance, leaving little room for self-preservation, fun and joy. Ultimately, it can pave the way to burnout and distract from one of the greatest adventures in life: getting to understand and accept who we are in our *wholeness*. The great bits. The silly bits. And the less bright bits.

> When changemaking becomes the singular lens through which we view ourselves, it can bring challenges.

So how do we cultivate an identity beyond "goodness", "virtue" or "changemaking", and why is that important for resilience? Your back might be up already, and you might notice yourself responding, "It's not that I choose to overidentify with changemaking, it's that nobody else is taking action and we're in an emergency." Totally, but have you considered that more people might join our movement if changemaking felt less stressed and more alive? "We don't have time for this – how privileged, how selfish", is a familiar narrative, and one that is no good for you, your sphere of influence and as I'll demonstrate, changemaking itself. "I don't have time or interest in something so vapid and self-interested as a personal life." I get it, and I have felt in my own journey the all-encompassing burden of the work. I have felt my internal eye be so judgemental that I couldn't indulge in life beyond "virtue". I couldn't give myself the permission to let go of guilt and embrace fun, joy and lightness. This chapter is *your* permission.

Humans First, Changemakers Second

I began my changemaking journey critical of unequal and unjust systems, trying to use my energy and life choices to actively resist them. That meant building "who am I" by deciding "who I am not". In a social media age of trying to squeeze our whole self into a Hinge profile or a social media bio, our "personhood" becomes one-dimensional. We are increasingly defined by causes and virtues. But identity isn't finite, it is expansive. You are more than a bio, you are more than a changemaker. You are at minimum a fleshy meat sack, responding to tens of thousands of inputs of data each day. At maximum, you are infinite possibility. You are a creature with hopes, desires, interests and preferences. You are not a set of conditions, but a meandering river: dropping sediment, picking things up, forging pathways, eroding others, sometimes polluted, but always a hospitable environment for an ecosystem of aliveness. You have a name and a location, but the waters of your river are ever changing, ever moving. In the words of eco-futurist Octavia Butler, "All that you touch you Change. All that you Change Changes you. The only lasting truth is Change."[24]

That's why in the first step of our eight-week programme, we ban the "c" word. In this case, it's climate. But for this book, it's changemaking. What might seem counterintuitive to a programme for youth concerned about climate is a route to meeting yourself liberated from the lens and scrutiny of "virtue". You are not expected to share who you campaign with, have a deep working knowledge of power and privilege or profile your devotion to feminist ecology. In this space of meeting strangers, you must hunt for who you are beyond the fight. Speak about your hobbies, your interests and your family. What sets you alight on your weekends? Who do you think of when you're sad? What do you cherish the most that you're protesting to protect?

When we present ourselves as whole individuals rather than activists on a mission, we invite genuine connection, empathy and potentially greater collaboration. From the outset, we are minimizing the urge to view others through a lens of competition, instead through one of shared humanity. We do this as a crucial step in trust-based community-building, which is essential to creating the parameters for vulnerable sharing and transformation (Guidepost 2). In the previous chapter I propose that the solution to imposter syndrome is authenticity. Being authentic in who we are, rather than performing as who we think we should be, creates a safer container to allow us to vocalize things like "I don't know the answer to that", and "I feel like I'm not doing enough." It offers us permission to grow, learn and change.

Let authenticity be the antidote to perfect.

Authenticity recognizes that changemaking and expertise are not grounded in a performance of knowledge or virtue but the feelings of caring, living and owning your story. You are an expert in the youth climate movement because you are young, and you've felt betrayed. You are an activist against human trafficking because you care deeply about gender justice and are taking a stand. You may not have all the answers. Why? Because you probably don't need to. You aren't an elected representative or a university lecturer or a specialist. This isn't to say that we shouldn't educate ourselves, we absolutely should. Read, listen, watch and learn from those outside your lived experience. Weave these learnings into your praxis and your approach. Continually iterate and change so that your work is uplifting others in the most meaningful way to them. But let authenticity be the antidote to perfect.

It is vital to recognize that we are multifaceted human beings with contradictions, imperfections and desires beyond changemaking. No one can maintain the impossible standard of unwavering purity or perfection. Engaging in interests and hobbies unrelated to your issue is not a betrayal of the cause. On the contrary, these pursuits are essential for creating balance and fostering joy. Whether it is exploring art, music, sports, travel or any other passion, these aspects of our lives provide much-needed energy and a renewed sense of purpose when we return to our changemaking. They allow us to connect with others on a human level, deepening relationships and building bridges with those who might initially feel distant from our political messages.

Who Would You Be in a Different Time or Space?

"Okay, so how do I figure out who I am?" That's a meaty question and one which will take a lifetime of unpicking. Two offerings for starting this process are imagining beyond the crises and finding "pointless" joy. For the former, stoking a holistic sense of identity involves asking ourselves, "Who would I be if the climate crisis/justice crisis did not exist?" It's a thought experiment to encourage us to imagine the parts of ourselves that might otherwise flourish if the world were free from different emergencies, which required mobilization. For example, if the climate crisis didn't exist, my vocation might be in fashion. I bought my first blazer when I was 15. I covered my childhood bedroom wall with pages from *Vogue*. But when I became an activist, I abandoned the blazers. I changed my relationship with fast fashion for the better, opting for second-hand and thrifted clothes, but I also changed my aesthetic to better fit into the collective. Formal wear was considered the uniform of the capitalists, and high-fashion gratuitous, so I switched the shirts for Dr Martens. Later in my journey, sustainable fashion influencers gave me permission to love fashion as an artistic pursuit rather than a vanity project. So, I started wearing suits again. I *love* a power suit – and didn't think I was allowed to. It felt like a betrayal of the cause. But feeling more comfortable in my skin, getting creative with my expression and channelling the power that suits unlock in me has given me the confidence to both push back and push forward. I no longer blend in. I'm present. I take up space.

Finding out who we are beyond changemaking is not leaving the fight but absorbing nutrients from the different places we plant ourselves. While this quest may not take into account the contexts we exist in (such as financial limitations), it invites us to dig into the place where we dream and reconnect with our values, interests and relationships. It's not to be framed as an exit from activism but a return to the self beneath it.

EXERCISE: WHO AM I?

Objective: Activism can become a kind of identity armour. Over time, we might begin to introduce ourselves by the causes we stand for, the systems we resist, the "isms" we reject. This exercise invites you to peel that back.

Step 1: Ban the "C" Word

For the next 30 minutes, our "c" word is changemaker. You're *not* a changemaker or an activist. Let that go for 30 minutes.

If you're doing this alone, journal about the following questions. If you're doing this in a group, journal for 20 minutes and then discuss it in pairs.

Step 2: Ask (and Answer)

Choose 5–7 of the following questions to reflect on. No pressure to be profound. Just be honest.

- What would I want to be doing with my life if the climate crisis didn't exist?
- What brings me fun, inspiration and excitement that has nothing to do with my cause?

- Who do I become when I'm completely relaxed?
- What kind of person do I want to be remembered as, not by history, but by my best friend?
- What parts of me have I stopped expressing since becoming a changemaker?
- What makes me laugh like an idiot?
- What's something totally unproductive I'd love to try?

Step 3: If You're in a Pair

Take turns sharing your answers for 10 minutes. Listen without fixing. Just witness. Celebrate the parts of each other that have nothing to do with being "good" or "productive".

Step 4: Come Back (Gently)

Reflect on how it felt to meet yourself outside of a role or cause. Was anything surprising? Did you feel resistance? Relief? A bit of both?

Step 5: Commitment

What's one way you can make space for these forgotten or undernourished parts of yourself? Commit to doing that this week for seven days.

By broadening our sense of self-worth, we build a strong foundation that protects us from collapsing under the weight of individual campaigns. If an initiative falls short or a policy change fails to materialize, it does not define us as failures. When we are grounded in diverse sources of fulfilment, we approach our activism with renewed energy and focus, free from the fear that every setback is a personal defeat. With an understanding of who we are and what we love, we can find more outlets for coping with stress.

Moreover, nurturing a broader identity – one which is nerdy or flawed or a gym fanatic – helps build connections within our movements. It creates the precedent for non-activism meet-ups such as craft days, Dungeons & Dragons clubs or wild swimming. Other examples for pursuits you could do together could include:

- Learning the hobbies of others. Make a rota so that everyone in your campaign group gets to offer a 15-minute lecture on something they love for example, trees, Marvel, baking, knitting. Engage with and celebrate them.
- Having monthly "non-activism" gatherings; for example, Extinction Rebellion Youth Bristol used to meet up for tree-climbing and bouldering. Fridays for Future Sweden created a "Spam" chat where they were able to speak about school. UKYCC did team-building exercises like online murder mystery games.

If you're a solo changemaker and not part of a cohesive group, you could:

- Give yourself permission to engage in activities "inside the system". Go to the cinema, eat out for dinner, read the latest cosy crime book.
- Dream up campaigns that weave together art, food and your hobbies *with* changemaking.

Seek Pointless Joy

A second suggestion for a pathway back to yourself is seeking pointless joy. A few years ago I was facilitating an eight-week programme with climate activists on burnout, with guest lecturer Lyndsay Burntonshaw. We were all between the ages of 16–24, sitting in a village hall discussing what brought us joy. In the first round of sharing, we all presented our hobbies. Some said "bouldering", others said "painting". But the longer we stayed in our sharing circle, the more answers shifted from traditional hobbies to genuine joy-based activities. One admitted, "To be honest, I used to love birdwatching, but now I go bouldering because my friends do it. I do enjoy it, but it's not totally just for me." Another confessed, through a muffled giggle, "To be really honest, what brings me joy is listening to One Direction." Then a cascade of bright honesty followed: "I love playing my flute", "I used to write poetry". It was here that the idea of pointless joy was born.

Resilience is often misunderstood as grit, endurance and the ability to keep going no matter the hardship. But psychological research and history alike reveal that resilience is deeply intertwined with joy. Neuroscientists have found that laughter and play activate the brain's reward system, reducing stress and reinforcing connection.[25] We may have all experienced that the human nervous system does not function well in a constant state of crisis. Movements survive not only because of strategy and sacrifice but because of the relationships, music, art, humour and shared connections that sustain them.

Historically, joy was often seen as a by-product of movements rather than a strategy. Protest songs were sung during the civil rights movement, and satirical postcards wove humour into the Suffragette campaigns. These moments show that joy was always present but not always acknowledged as essential. The shift became more explicit in the late 20th century, as activist communities reckoned with burnout. Indigenous resistance movements drew on longstanding traditions to weave storytelling, music and ceremony into their organizing, recognizing that cultural joy was inseparable from political survival. Anti-globalization protests in the 1990s introduced creative forms of direct action, from dance parties to carnival-like demonstrations. LGBTQ+ Pride parades began centring celebration as a tool for defiance. These echo in the tactics of modern campaigns. For example, in 2018 Extinction Rebellion transformed Waterloo Bridge in London into a "garden bridge" by filling it with foliage. Here, against the backdrop of environmental collapse, I sang songs, watched hula hoop dancers and saw people laughing.

Pointless joy distinguishes between conventional joy and what we do for joy, simply for the sake of it. In a society where we are weighed by our productivity, I'm taken by the idea of pointlessness. Changemaking is full of purpose and points. There is always a social media asset to be created, a campaign to operationalize or a problem to fix. It sits in a broader capitalism context, where focus has become less about the pursuit of truth and more about attainment, aspiration and achievement – follower growth, gross domestic product and climbing the ladder. Pointlessness, therefore, feels like *reclamation* of our time, rather than its commodification.

I started my own practice in pointlessness by making giant recreations of food. With my best friend, we'd bookmark a day at the weekend and bake huge and ridiculous versions of food, at home. Our niche was chocolate bars. What may seem a laughable jolly became a spiritual endeavour. It was pointless for several reasons. Firstly, the end product tastes average at best but, realistically, poor. Have you ever tried to boil a giant, single piece of ravioli? You end up with a sad pile of raw-ish pasta. And an enormous belly full of laughs. Secondly, it took hours to make and after a day, all I had left was photos and memories. I didn't try to sell my creations, create an Instagram reel or monetize them. Among others I made a giant KitKat Chunky, a giant Crunchie (honeycomb candy covered in chocolate) and a giant Bourbon biscuit, known as the "bourboy".

The deeper question I got to explore here was: what do I do, not for productivity but because it brings me joy and lightness *for the sake of it*? Of all the things I do, what am I doing for *me*, rather than to improve my dinner conversation, to be more interesting, to have a more alluring dating profile or improve my social status. While I enjoy podcasts, deep dives into the news, rock climbing and watching indie films, they have glimmers of productive value. Whereas making a giant chocolate bar? Not at all. What that does is dial up the fun, imagination and creativity.

It can be difficult to remove ourselves from the social matrix to interrogate what we do for ourselves and what we do, in part, for others. So here is a shortcut. What did you enjoy when you were a kid? Here, you were less concerned about your social status and more concerned with doing things that you really enjoyed. I used to write poems about bugs, play the recorder, design clothes, write stories and make videos with my pals. I fundamentally still love all these things, yet I make little space for them because they don't contribute to my sense of productivity.

The first part of our reset is to uncover the human beneath the changemaker, recognize where we may feel impoverished and decide on our own unique and authentic ways to address our deficiencies. This involves scrutiny and analysis of a bigger question: Who Am I? And it involves recognizing that joy and lightness don't negate the struggle but fortify those within it. As feminist Emma Goldman put it, "If I can't dance it's not my revolution." In simple terms, joy *is* productive because it reminds us who we are and what we're trying to preserve for future generations. It enables our sense of vitality, where momentum, radiance, imagination and life exist. To be a changemaker is not just to fight but to live; to dance in protest, to build movements that are not just about dismantling the old but imagining and embodying the new. Joy is not a luxury; it is an act of resistance. And perhaps, the most radical thing we can do is to insist on it.

EXERCISE: FINDING POINTLESS JOY

Objective: Before algorithms, CVs and Instagram, there was you – with all your weird, unmarketable passions. Let's meet them again.

Step 1: Journalling

- What did you enjoy doing as a child?

Write down at least three memories that bring a sense of that childlike delight back into your body.

- What do you do that secretly serves your image, ambition or social status more than your joy?
- What do you love doing even though it makes you "less interesting" at parties or other social gatherings?
- What's something you've stopped doing because it seemed silly, unproductive or pointless?

List two activities you've dropped because they didn't feel "useful enough". Do you miss them?

- What brings you joy and lightness, *for the sake of it*?
- What is your pointless joy?

Step 2: Commitment

Pick one thing you're going to do this week that is entirely, unapologetically pointless. Something you do just because it makes you feel alive, absurd or connected to something tender.

Some ideas:

- Write a stupid song
- Build a fairy house in the garden and leave it there
- Do cartwheels and handstands in the park.
- Play the Sims or other games.
- Build a blanket fort in your bedroom.
- Make your own giant pizza.
- Have your friends over for a jam session.
- Find and gather sticks in the forest. Place them on top of each other. See how many you can balance until your construction falls apart.

The pointless thing you choose to do doesn't need to be Instagrammable. In fact, better if it's not. This is a private revolution.

CHAPTER 6: GUIDEPOST 2 – THE POWER OF PEER SUPPORT

"Rarely, if ever, are any of us healed in isolation. Healing is an act of communion."[26]

bell hooks

I was once invited to deliver a one-hour workshop at an international conference on inner development in Sweden. This was a huge deal to me. I'd be inside a historic church speaking to 600 people in person, and thousands more who were joining online. The Resilience Project was moving through a funding crisis and I knew that this was my last shot to find the funding necessary for our continuation. So, it became one of the biggest speaking opportunities I'd had to date. But life had a different plan for me.

The week before, to pacify the stress building in my body and mind, I carved out space for going to the gym and yoga. These are two tools in my Resilience Rucksack (Guidepost 6) to tame stress and balance my breathing; one speeds me up and the other slows me down. But one week before the talk I woke up screaming in pain, unable to lift my head from the pillow without spasms ricocheting from my neck. I stayed still, ingesting pain relief from a horizontal position and texting my team to let them know that I'd be unable to work. When I was finally able to get to the doctor – yes, in my pyjamas – she explained that I'd suffered a shoulder injury. I was surprised, because there was nothing too strenuous about my exercise, which I had been doing for a while. Though I'd kept doing the same moves, I was showing up in a different state. My body was a cave of stress, with nerves, overwhelm and adrenaline stitching themselves into my muscle fibres. All that bracing and tensing had led to a frozen shoulder.

With the assistance of some gnarly pain medication, I spent the next five days drifting in and out of sleep, forced to sleep upright with my arm in a sling. I directed my eyes toward a TV screen and away from the fact that the biggest talk of my life was in four days' time, and I'd lost a week's worth of prep. Inevitably, the perfectionist saboteurs in my mind starting yelling, "You're going to F this up", "You're going to humiliate yourself" and, "You're not good enough." I had two options. Either I could let the voices win and I could cancel the talk, even though I would physically be able to stand on stage. Or I could surrender to imperfection by finding out not what "perfect" but what "good enough" looks like. But being good enough would not result in going viral, securing more funding or getting a standing ovation. Good enough would be showing up and bravely stepping on stage, rather than cancelling for fear of embarrassment. The win would be to show up as I was, to allow myself to be messy and to acknowledge that sometimes life has a different plan for you. So, on I went.

With a sling, pain medication filling my pockets and an unconvincing "can-do" attitude, I got myself to Sweden, forced to own that I was underprepared and overwhelmed. On the morning of the talk, I woke up knowing that part of the workshop was as much a mystery to me as it was to the audience. The known parts were my introduction and introducing a paired practice of "active listening" for five minutes. This exercise – detailed at the end of this chapter – invites a pair of people to answer the same question while listening deeply, with Person A going first and Person B going second and no discussion or feedback in between. The goal of the listener is to quieten the inner monologue of their mind, resisting the urge to comment and say, "Oh yes, I can relate because …", and *truly* listen to someone else. As the speaker, the goal is to embrace the rare opportunity to speak uninterrupted in a stream of consciousness and not be guided by someone else's response or further questioning. In speaking for a length of time and overcoming the discomfort of being witnessed in our entirety, we may be surprised to see what comes out of our mouth, and what's been hiding inside us behind polite conversational etiquette. In my introduction I would use data and testimonials from our work to showcase the almost divine, revelatory and soothing impact of being seen, heard and understood by others. I wanted to drive home the message that our answer to the climate crisis could lie in the shared humanity we can salvage from peer support and collective healing.

The audience participation in this exercise was important for me. To have faith in a concept we need to alchemize in our bodies, not just in our minds. Embodied wisdom, the learning we gather from how we are made to feel, is a far greater teacher than statistics and logic alone. For example, the unwavering and non-sensical commitment I have to Sheffield Wednesday Football Club has been alchemized through years of shared wins and losses with others. The value of my best friend is not rooted in her job or her salary or how often she texts me, but in years of shared tears and the feeling of mutual connection, trust and love.

The problem was, I hadn't yet decided what question I would be asking the audience to use to tap into this connection and shared reverence, and now my workshop was in two hours' time. I thought through some questions that could encourage us all to dig a little deeper, such as: *What's standing in the way of you being your biggest, brightest self? What does the world look like to you in 15 years' time? What do you wish for your children?* These questions are important, but they felt too enormous, too extensive. I didn't know what to ask, and sometimes when I don't know the answer, it feels more pertinent to hand it over to something bigger than myself. To this day, this is one of my most "am-I-having-a-breakdown?" moments. Maybe it was fatigue or the strong pain medication I was on for my shoulder, but I went and spoke to a tree. I walked out of the venue and found the biggest, wisest looking tree and sat beside it. I asked the tree, "Oh wise one, Oh one of hundreds of years of seeing and witnessing, Oh one of exceptional listening capacity, what should I ask the audience today?" I waited for a voice that I knew wouldn't come, for words unable to be articulated. And inside me, I heard the tree whisper back, "How are you?"

My inner saboteurs laughed in delight, "You can't stand on an international stage alongside some of the most infamous international speakers in neuroscience and inner development and offer: 'How are you?' I could go to the shops, to the bus stop, to the doctor and be asked that question – I hear it ten times a day. But at a conference I've paid to attend, I'm looking for something a bit more profound!" Suppressing these voices, trusting the tree and having close to no time to think the decision through properly, I walked back into the church and waited the final 15 minutes before my slot. I took a deep breath and walked on stage. The last thing I heard was the rush of blood pulsating through my brain and the host in my ear whispering, "Katie, rock them!"

I got up on that stage in my best suit and spoke through my work for about 40 minutes, approaching the moment of vulnerability at speed. I took a breath, declaring honestly that I'd been mulling over what to ask them all morning but neglecting to share that I was now following the advice of an oak tree. I shared that we'd be exploring three very simple words: "How are you?" and began instructing the audience how to do the exercise.

I was accompanied by a pianist during the talk, who started softly playing music as strangers reshuffled to pair up and begin an eye-gazing exercise: staring into each other's eyes for a few minutes in the hope they could really start *seeing* each other. What started as muffled giggles and fidgeting quickly settled into what I can only think of as magic. I was profoundly moved to see strangers with tears in their eyes, smiling. My saboteurs tried to creep in, commenting, "Wow, and now you're crying on stage" but I was too distracted by the wave of awe spreading across me. I then invited the pairs to answer the simple, yet powerful question "How are you?" They each had five minutes to answer the question without interruption.

In closing the exercise I saw people wiping tears, hugging and exchanging phone numbers. I opened space for feedback afterwards and it was overwhelmingly positive. Some felt it had deepened their roots of connection and others that it was "incredible" how moved they had been by having asked and answered such a simple question. Another commented that it had allowed her to feel like a "majestic tree". At the end, I received that standing ovation.

Vulnerability: Our Untapped Superpower

Sharing how we truly are, be that full of sorrow and hopelessness or inspired and deeply motivated, is letting ourselves and others in on the secret of what it means to be alive. "How are you?" is not just a greeting, it is a doorway – a doorway to more than just taking action without burning out. Every changemaker, who may appear to be a superhero to the watching world, possesses the soft underbelly of a sensitive human being. Our underbelly is our most vulnerable part, but not our weakest. It's one of our greatest sources of strength, because vulnerability breeds connection and mutual understanding. To see each one of us with a soft underbelly –

We share a common desire to feel witnessed, seen and supported by others.

wants, needs, insecurities and fragilities – creates kinder changemaking spaces where we are less inclined to shame each other for not doing enough. Beyond our justified rage, our chosen fights, our chosen tactics and our location in the world, we share a common desire to feel witnessed, seen and supported by others.

In my journey to uncover the answers to some questions such as: *Who protects the protectors? Who cares for the carers? Who transforms those transforming?* I have found that "How are you?" – simple and concise – is a doorway to the support and connection we need as humans first, then changemakers. It extends our pronounced sense of global care to each other and ourselves. Through deeply listening and revealing vulnerability, we can find magic, connection, humanity and togetherness, which is the rich terrain of movements and mutual aid – the lining of history books.

"How are you?" may also bring discomfort and unease. For some people of a particular gender, culture, faith, class or upbringing, the expression of vulnerability is discouraged, punished or socially sanctioned. Undoing that work or unlearning those narratives won't happen in one exercise. It becomes important to develop patience, grow a language for discomfort and fundamentally only to unpack things that you feel you can safely repack afterwards. This mean understanding your emotional boundaries and whether or not sharing some things is more productive with a clinical professional.

In our work we talk about "creative discomfort" or "growing a taste for discomfort". This looks like nudging up to the line of your perceived comfort level, gently prodding it and getting curious about how moving that line may feel. To give an example, at retreats I've hosted I've had changemakers come with a predefined boundary line on opening up, not because they weren't strong enough to let their pain see the light, but because vulnerability is effing scary. Through gentle and loving encouragement, I saw them share things they've never spoken about before and the resulting liberation and levity. Imagine holding a stone in your hand with your arms outstretched. Holding it for ten minutes would be manageable. Holding it for 20 might start getting uncomfortable. Imagine holding the stone for days or weeks. It would start to feel extraordinarily heavy, and it would cause pain. Imagine holding the stone for years, and the heaviness with which you'd walk. Sometimes our fear of vulnerability can keep us holding the stone inside in the darkness. When we offer our stories to the light, through supported sharing, we can see them more clearly and see that they perhaps weren't as scary or shameful as we perceived.

Growing a taste for discomfort is an unavoidable learning of resilience and, in a society of great convenience, we're not trained for it. Changemaking as a discipline is profoundly uncomfortable; challenging power hierarchies and tipping the balance is thoroughly uncomfortable. Practising discomfort within our inner landscape, in an active listening exercise with people we trust, only serves to further develop our ability to hold discomfort in our external world.

Finally, it's often difficult to distinguish between healthy vulnerability and over-sharing or trauma-dumping. While vulnerability fosters intimacy, trust and understanding, unchecked emotional expression can sometimes overwhelm others, leaving them feeling burdened rather than connected. True vulnerability is about building bridges, not barriers. At its core, practising vulnerability means sharing personal experiences in an intentional and thoughtful way, as I will outline in the active listening exercise at the end of this chapter. It involves self-awareness, mutual respect and emotional containment, offering parts of yourself to others in a way that strengthens relationships rather than placing undue weight on them. Healthy vulnerability occurs in spaces where trust has been established, for example through the eye-gazing, and it allows for a reciprocal exchange so that both people feel emotionally safe and engaged. On the other hand, over-sharing often lacks context and emotional regulation. It may involve revealing deeply personal details without considering the relationship, the setting or the listener's readiness to receive such information. This kind of unfiltered sharing doesn't consider the boundaries or emotional needs of others. While vulnerability invites connection, over-sharing can feel like an emotional flood, leaving the listener unsure of how to respond. Trauma-dumping takes over-sharing one step further. It happens when someone unloads heavy emotional content onto another without their consent or consideration of their emotional capacity. Unlike healthy vulnerability, which seeks connection, trauma-dumping often seeks relief, with little regard for how the listener might be impacted. The person sharing may not yet have processed their own emotions and, rather than seeking true support, may instead be looking for an immediate emotional release.

To practise healthy, intentional vulnerability, it's important to consider three key questions before sharing:

- Is this the right time, place and person for this conversation?
- Is my sharing respecting the other person's emotional boundaries?
- Am I sharing from a place of reflection rather than impulse?

Checking in with these simple questions ensures that vulnerability remains a bridge to deeper understanding rather than an emotional weight placed on another. One of the easiest ways to navigate this fine line is by inviting, rather than imposing, deep emotional conversations. Additionally, developing strategies to self-regulate emotions before sharing, through journalling, self-reflection or professional support, ensures that vulnerability remains a tool for connection rather than an act of emotional unloading. In all endeavours, seek not to be a dump truck – be a fork-lift.

Peer Support, Resilience and the Majestic Tree

In 1930s Ohio, two men stumbled into each other's lives. One was Bill Wilson, a once-successful New York stockbroker whose love affair with booze had torpedoed his career and his happiness. The other was Dr Bob Smith, a talented but similarly self-destructive surgeon, spiralling through his own battles. Bill hit rock bottom countless times, but it is reported that something changed during one of his hospital stays. He is said to have had a profound spiritual moment, courtesy of the Oxford Group, a movement preaching personal change through spiritual practices. Armed with a new outlook but teetering on the edge of relapse, Bill needed someone who understood what he was going through. In an attempt to stay sober while away on business in Akron, Bill ended up in contact with Dr Bob through a mutual connection from the Oxford Group. What followed was a marathon heart-to-heart about drinking, addiction and life. Instead of judgement, they found a bond in mutual struggle and, for the first time, sobriety seemed not just possible but shared. Fuelled by coffee and conversations, the duo decided that this was too good not to share. Over time, they honed a set of principles based on what worked for them – honesty, accountability and a little spiritual hope. What started as two guys helping each other out snowballed into a worldwide movement that changed lives. This is the story of Alcoholics Anonymous (AA), the 12-step programme and their weekly peer support meetings.

I first heard the story of Bill and Bob through my inspiring mother-in-law, almost 100 years after their fateful cup of coffee. Through weekly meetings, she now has 18 years of sobriety and credits AA for changing her life. Her story is shared. As of 2023, there were 123,000 AA groups across approximately 180 countries, serving almost 2 million people globally.[27] The proof? Peer support and embracing vulnerability – to share, to ask for help, to bring our pain to light – is not an optional extra to a balanced life. It's proven as fundamental in supporting sobriety, overcoming addiction and maintaining positive mental health. The AA are one of the most prolific and promising examples of peer support and mutual aid, but there are many more, for mothers, men and now, for activists.

Resilience is built by: feeling seen, heard and understood (practising vulnerability in a community).

Inspired by Bob and Bill, and the learnings from the peer support in our Resilience Circles, the "resilience formula" below articulates how we begin our journey.

To break this down, we build emotional resilience through peer support, when we practise vulnerability, in a supportive and trusted community. It works because it:

1. Normalizes struggle. Peer support reduces feelings of isolation and shame. For example, hearing "me too" or "I've felt that way" in response to feelings of hopelessness reminds us that we are neither alone nor the anomaly. Hearing parts of our own story in others normalizes emotional difficulty as part of life and not as personal failure.
2. Promotes emotional safety. When someone listens without judgement or fixing, it soothes the nervous system and creates a sense of safety. It allows us to process emotions more fully, which enhances our capacity to handle future stressors.
3. Encourages self-reflection and growth. Listening deeply to others and being listened to in return, creates a reflective space. Here we can nurture emotional insights into why we feel certain ways, helping us in the future to identify patterns and coping strategies.
4. Builds communities of connection. Strong social bonds are among the most consistent predictors of resilience. Peer support cultivates a sense of belonging, helping you to feel anchored during periods of instability or hardship. In the

inevitable ebbs and flows of life, you might not remember the acronym you learned to deal with burnout in a workshop, but you will be able to WhatsApp someone in your community to talk it through with. Reading this book will help minimize burnout but utilizing it as an invitation to speak more openly with others and building communities of care will transform your life.

5. Reminds us of the miracle of others. This is your invitation to don your miracle goggles. Peer support helps us to see other changemakers not as competitors or saboteurs, but as miracles in their own right. They are a miracle for caring and devoting their time to the cause. They could be donating their gifts to entirely selfish pursuits or working for the fossil fuel lobby. Instead, they are here with you on the fringes of change with their own struggles, desires and insecurities. That doesn't mean they aren't flawed – we all are – but see them first through miracle goggles. It will bring you closer to others.

The eight-week model found that community, particularly an open, safe space where people can feel heard and validated, reduced feelings of loneliness and increased feelings of positive mental health.[28] Participants highlighted the importance of communities of care, recognizing that collective action is more effective than going it alone. We now have a validated mandate that leading from our feelings is not a weakness or a distraction, but an effective method for both flourishing as a human and effective activism.

Sitting in vulnerability is not easy. It involves imperfection, honesty, exposure, discomfort and unlearning. But it also includes connection, support, strength and resilience. Like my friend the oak tree, trees develop strong and deeper root systems through exposure to wind and other environmental stressors. It's a process known as "stress-induced strengthening" and happens when a tree reinforces its own structure in response to adversity. When trees are exposed to wind, their trunks and branches sway. This movement signals to the tree to grow stronger, deeper and more widespread roots to anchor itself. In the absence of wind, trees grow tall but weak. Without wind stress, they fail to develop the necessary structural strength. Engaging with vulnerability and the remaining six guideposts of this book will routinely ask you to sit in and embrace discomfort. But in doing so, your own stress-induced strengthening will begin, and you too can become the Majestic Tree.

EXERCISE: ACTIVE LISTENING AND EMOTIONAL HEALTH CHECKS

Objective: This exercise is designed to be conducted in pairs, with your campaigning group, your friends, your housemate, your child or members of your family. It aims to deepen connection, cultivate emotional awareness and deliver peer support through the practice of active listening. Participants take turns answering the question "How are you?" while the other person listens without interruption, feedback or judgement.

Active listening is the practice of fully concentrating, understanding and listening to what another person is saying without interrupting, judging or formulating a response while they speak. It requires the listener to be present, minimize internal and external distractions, and provide non-verbal cues of attentiveness, such as maintaining eye contact and nodding.

Materials needed:

- A timer (phone, watch or clock)
- A quiet space where pairs can converse without distractions
- Optional: a notebook each for post-exercise reflections

Step One: Setting the scene (5 minutes)

- Sit in a quiet and private setting.
- State and ensure that this is a safe, non-judgemental space where each person has the opportunity to be fully heard.

Step Two: Eye-gazing

- Pair up, preferably with someone you don't know well and, while sitting relatively close to each other, look into each other's eyes in silence for 1 minute.
- This is uncomfortable, so expect some smiling, giggling or fidgeting. Try to just sit in this discomfort and quieten your mind.

Accessibility check: eye-gazing can be uncomfortable for everyone, but particularly those who are neurodivergent. If anyone in your group has an expression of neurodivergence such as autism, they can place their hands opposite each other, facing upward, with fingers close to nearly touching their partner's, instead of gazing into each other's eyes. Hand-gazing demands an equal amount of attention.

Step Three: Establish Roles and Guidelines

- Decide who is going to speak and who will listen first. Person A becomes the first speaker and Person B the first listener.
- Remind the listener to:
    - Resist the urge to respond or interject with personal experiences.
    - Focus fully on the speaker's words, maintaining eye contact if comfortable.
    - Notice their own internal reactions and thoughts without acting on them.

- Remind the speaker to:
  - Speak freely, following their train of thought without filtering.
  - Embrace pauses and moments of reflection.
  - Welcome silence if that's required. Silence is okay.
  - Avoid self-editing or worrying about how they sound.

Step Four: Begin the Exercise (10 minutes)

- Start the timer for five minutes.
- Person A speaks while Person B listens attentively.
- Once the time is up, allow a few seconds of silence before switching roles.
- Repeat with Person B speaking and Person A listening for five minutes.

Step Five: Reflection (10 minutes)

- Use the following questions for reflection:
  - How did it feel to be truly listened to?
  - What was challenging about staying silent and resisting the urge to respond?
  - What did you notice about your own thoughts and reactions?

Final Note: Integrate active listening into your daily life, whether in personal conversations, meetings or moments of support with friends and colleagues.

CHAPTER 7: GUIDEPOST 3 – LET YOUR FEELINGS EAT

The Guest House
This body, O youth, is a guest-house:
every morning a new guest comes running.
Beware, do not say, "The (guest) is a burden to me,"
for presently it will fly back into non-existence.
Whatsoever comes into thy heart
from the invisible world is thy guest:
entertain it well![29]

Rumi

We are overwhelmed and overstimulated by things that shouldn't *be*: the glow of constant LED lighting, the exorbitant wealth of billionaires, the mercilessness of war, the apathy of our elected leaders. And we have enabled things our ancestors once strived for: choice, chemotherapy, the belief that we can seize any and every opportunity, a larger pool of potential life partners. The carousel of emotions that modern living exposes us to can move us from gratitude and awe in the morning, to burnout in the afternoon. Put simply, it's an emotionally volatile time to be alive and our statistics reflect that. We are having a lot more "Big Feelings", and these feelings now have big names. As mentioned, rates of depression and anxiety have risen by 25 per cent globally since the COVID-19 pandemic.[30] In the UK, the likelihood of young people aged 5 to 16 experiencing a mental health problem has risen by 50 per cent over the past three years.[31] In the US, in 2023, 40 per cent of high school students reported feeling so sad or hopeless for two weeks or more in a row that they had stopped doing some of their usual activities in the past 12 months.[32]

In a clinical setting, these names and diagnoses are both fundamental to getting the correct support and validating our experiences. However, much mental health rhetoric now comes from those who are not professionals, with a rise of self-diagnosis of mental health conditions through social media rather than GP referrals.[33,**] While self-diagnosis may feel helpful to the individual and override the eye-watering waiting lists for meaningful support, it can amplify the idea that there are "good" and "bad" feelings, creating a strict emotional hierarchy that leaves us craving some states and feeling shame for others. This hierarchy is emboldened by capitalism and individualism, with the social narrative running that if you're sad, you're not productive, which makes you unworthy. In fact, sadness might be the appropriate response to your given life circumstances. Sadness might be an important container to sit in for a while. We aren't taught hold to hold sadness. So, we compare ourselves to others and feel shame that something is wrong with us, adding unwanted layers of complexity to the picture. We feel emotions *about* the emotions. That's a lot to hold.

Another complexity is the narrative that the Big Feeling is a life sentence, encouraging a modality that we "are" something rather than it being a temporary guest in our home. For example, we might say, "I have social anxiety", rather than, "I feel anxious among new people I haven't built trust with", or, "I have depression", rather than a more amusing take like, "I am in a season of great emotional decline". Words carry power and impact our sense of resilience. Using language to signify that we embody one emotional state misunderstands us as humans with different parts. One part of us might feel

** A survey reported by Tebra indicated that 1 in 4 people had diagnosed themselves with an illness based on information found on social media. Among these, 48 per cent self diagnosed with anxiety, and 37 per cent with depression.

anxious when we speak in large groups, but another part of us might feel exceptionally confident with those we love. "I am . . . " robs us of the many ways we show up and the potential for experiencing multiple emotions simultaneously, or "both/and". You can feel anxious in life *and* feel a great sense of strength in who you are. You can feel depressed about the world *and* experience joy in the moments of your day. Emotions can co-exist.***

During my second burnout (see Chapter 12), the sadness felt so consuming that I had no clear roadmap of how to continue functioning on a daily basis. I remember telling my housemate that I didn't know if I'd ever feel happiness again. We might want to label this quickly as depression, though stating that without a clinical diagnosis corrupted the truth to me that my body and emotional landscape were responding naturally to shock. There was a way forward where I could have felt both *depressed* and *well* at the same time. My friend Joey suggested that I could carry the feelings of depression around with me like I was carrying them around in a bag, rather than hiding away with my ailment. It was my accessory, rather than me entirely. So, I changed my story: I didn't have clinical depression; rather, life had handed me a great chunk of sadness that I now dutifully carried with me. That meant I could still live my life, find soft laughter and connection, navigating the bag, rather than shutting my life down entirely. I could adjust to my new normal and know that depression would enjoy its stay at my guest house and move on in time.

Anxiety is another good example here. I write about resilience *and* I suffer from panic attacks. After a period without them for almost ten years, last year the weight of leading an international organization, the fundraising, the team management and the public speaking, resulted in more panic attacks. They would come from nowhere. I'd be speaking about the work we do and

*** I speak here outside the clinical environment, as I am not a mental health practitioner, therapist or doctor.

suddenly the world would spin, my heart would beat rapidly and I felt like I was going to die. My first thought was that I had an anxiety disorder, which led me to say no to a few public speaking opportunities. When I started to self-limit because of an idea of who I was and what I had, I finally asked myself, "At this point, do I *have* anxiety, or does anxiety have me?" Having panic attacks and anxiety, rather than a diagnosis, was a signal for me to slow down and make big changes in my life. It was a reminder that stress leaves its mark on your nervous system and there is sometimes no mind hack you can do to overcome physical symptoms. I needed to make the changes to re-regulate my nervous system. Anxiety was an unwelcome guest, but one with something to tell me: that I still care what people think of me, that I work a bit too hard, that running makes me feel great but doesn't downregulate my system, and that unproductive rest is essential. So, accept the speaking gig, do the scary thing, share your mind in class – feel utterly nervous, maybe even fuck up – and be okay with that. Anxiety may be a part of you, but it's not *all* of you.

Anxiety may be a part of you, but it's not *all* of you.

Our next guidepost in building resilience is to redesign our relationship to our emotions, counterintuitively saying yes to our vast – and sometimes uncomfortable – emotional landscape. Changemaking, or stepping into the Arena, is a vantage point for seeing both the best and the worst of humanity. It is volatile, perilous and involves both life and death. It is likely then that you will nudge close to the biggest emotions a human can hold. Depression, yes. Anxiety, absolutely. In trying to do good you will sometimes end up feeling very bad. And that too is okay.

The Emotional Banquet

Picture all your emotions gathering like a council to discuss the happenings of your internal landscape. If you've seen *Inside*

Out, you might already imagine your council of emotional archetypes, all with differing ideas on how to respond to any given situation at any given moment. In embracing emotional diversity, I introduce the Emotional Banquet.**** Imagine that all your emotions – Jealousy, Grief, Rage, Compassion, Anxiety, Joy, Apathy, Sadness and so on – are all invited to a feast. At one end of the table sits Rage, already irritated by the unnecessary amount of cutlery (who needs two forks and who is paying for this?!). Next to them sits Grief, staring idlily at her plate. At the other end of the table you'll find Despair, curled inside herself, chewing her nails as if that's the appetizer. Someone nudges their chair an inch closer to Despair and gently whispers, "How has your morning been?" It's Compassion. Next to them sits Joy, unperturbed that today's menu is full of cheese – and they're vegan.

Around this table, each of your emotions is offered a seat. There is no hierarchy. All the guests are invited to share a meal. At a civil banquet, the etiquette holds that each guest serves themselves an equitable amount of food to ensure that everyone gets fed, all are nourished and no one goes hungry. But these guests are not well practised. You can think of a meal as an event that happens to you from the large to the small. At your Emotional Banquet, countless meals are served a day; sometimes these are enormous meals, such as when we go through a major life event; and other are smaller meals like feeling helpless about global tragedy; or a snack, like a difficult exchange with your campaign mate. Imagine a campaign you have poured your heart into doesn't get the traction you were hoping for. Dinner is served, but before the food even gets to the table, Despair, Anger and Hopelessness have leaped over their chairs to consume it all. Hope, Joy and Inspiration are left hungry.

Inevitably, this will happen many times in our lives. Voracious hunger can take over some of our emotions,

**** This concept has been iterated from Caroline Hickman's idea of embracing our emotional biodiversity.

particularly Anxiety and Anger, leaving no sustenance for Joy. Sometimes they need to eat the lion's share. Sometimes they deserve to. But when this happens frequently, we run into trouble. If Anxiety is always eating the majority of our life sustenance, not only will we generally feel atrocious, but other emotions like Joy, Inspiration and Hope become starved. Their power begins to wither and their ability to inform and influence our decisions is inhibited. Conversely, we might be a changemaker where Hope is eating all the food, leaving none for the others for fear that they will grow strong enough to debilitate us. Without allowing Grief, Despair and Sadness also to eat, we could fall into naïve optimism, where we uncritically believe that things will be okay. This phenomenon is called "emotional bypass", a coping mechanism that involves avoiding, ignoring or suppressing uncomfortable emotions to protect ourselves.

The power of the metaphor is such that every emotion deserves a plate at the banquet, and we run into trouble when one emotion, or a collection of similar emotions, start to eat more than their fair share. If only Hopelessness is eating, he will grow bigger and larger and crowd out all else. We might find that this then leads to mental health challenges such as clinical depression or anxiety. Instead, Hopelessness gets a plate, and on occasion a much bigger plate, because he is a welcome guest at our table. Like Rumi's powerful poem "The Guest House" (see page 89), the Emotional Banquet attempts to normalize and celebrate each guest. At the dinner of your mind, each has something to reveal to you. In response to the events of our lives and the world, it is appropriate that a variety of emotions need to eat. They all have something to say, something to offer and they are invited to sit in your council and say their piece. They all have needs: Grief needs witnessing, Joy needs companionship, Sadness needs connection. If we can treat emotions as guests at

This is not a book about denying your emotions, it's about hosting them.

our banquet or guests in our house, uncomfortable or difficult emotions are no longer problems we need to correct. Instead, understanding their needs becomes part of the art of hosting. This is not a book about denying your emotions, it's about hosting them.

Fight the Dragon, Get the Gold

The binary thinking that there are strictly good emotions and bad emotions is a Western fallacy. Rather, some emotions may be more or less *serving* to our mental health, our campaign work and our relationships. To give an example, Guilt is a prominent and hungry emotion in changemaking. We feel guilty about our lifestyle choices, for not doing enough, for not engaging with the news enough, for moving on too quickly from tragedy or for being inconsistent with allyship. But in some framings, Guilt can be an appropriate response to a situation. It can nudge action, prompt conversations and engender apologies. It can be a positive driver. In other ways, it can stifle action, encourage shame and lead to retreat. Rumi's invitation is that each emotion-guest, just as the people you bring into your home, has some aspects you relish and others that can feel challenging. So here Guilt becomes an enquiry rather than a debilitating state: someone with questions. What does Guilt want and what does Guilt *need?* Guilt might need to take positive action on some days and require reassurance on others that we can't do or be everything.

When we do the uncomfortable work of saying yes to emotions, we understand that they too have many different sides. After years of unstitching the belief that Anger sits ugly with women, it has become one of my most treasured emotions. The fire that lives inside Anger is one of many identities. Fire can be for energy, activation and creation, like that of the hearth. Its ability to create things, make food and warmth fosters hospitable environments for people to gather. This kind of fire, with its boundless energy and gathering potential, is a great attribute for leaders, creators, builders and changemakers. But another fire, an uncontrollable blaze, can become destructive, spreading quickly and causing people to flee. Fire, or Anger, require both oxygen and control in managed doses – or for our banquet analogy, food. Too much food and our fire could cause harm, leading to burnout. Too little food and our fire could become extinguished. Too little control and our fire could cause damage. Too much control and our fire could become suppressed. As Black Feminist Audre Lorde speaks on Anger, "My response to racism is anger. That anger has eaten clefts into my living only when it remained unspoken, useless to anyone." Anger needs to be spoken with, understood, transformed and used as fuel for action. Without, we host a banquet where some gorge and others are starved. No wonder I ended up with an eating disorder.

Despair as the Chrysalis for Hope

In witnessing that so-called "bad" emotions did not end me or break me but made me stronger, I learned that befriending all emotions is a vehicle for resilience. Understanding rather than rejecting these emotions means that you can process them (and not be consumed by them) the next time they arise. You can bat emotions away for years but eventually they will confiscate that bat and arrive, unexpected and uninvited, at your front door.

Befriending these emotions has made me a better changemaker as I can more easily sit with pervasive loss and not be debilitated. The 73 per cent decline of global wildlife populations in the last 50 years and the murder of an environmental activist every other day in 2023, are two examples of heartbreaking loss we must confront.[34,35] While it may feel bleak to read, and emotional states can arrive with a seemingly never-ending intensity, emotional states are not a life sentence.

To take an example, hidden within Despair is momentum. At a collective level, it moves me away from the small happenings of my own life and plugs me straight back into the reality bigger than myself. It connects me again with my why – why am I doing this? Why am I choosing the path of change? Because of the things that should *not* be. Truly looking at injustice has propelled me into outrage and action, mobilization and strategy. Without a strong connection to my why, my choices for positive impact might be sporadic, seasonal and temporary, rather than the guiding principles of my life. At a personal level, understanding despair invites me to think through how I can minimize its potency for others. It inspires a resolve in me that if I can't change these massive global happenings tomorrow, then instead each day I can try to model humanity's innate goodness. I can engage in small and random acts of kindness as a reminder to myself and others that we as a humanity are not eternally lost, we are simply temporarily misguided. This process for me certainly isn't instant. I often need to sit with despair, seek peer support, then get scheming.

Hidden within despair is momentum.

This momentum, just like that of a pendulum swing, moves me toward connection with others first, then action, then potentially to hope. Conversely, the pendulum can also move back. Staying in hope can feel so buoyant and transformative that devastating world news or setbacks give a sense of whiplash. You may feel you've misunderstood where we are as a world. You may feel alienated and disconnected and move back to despair. This emotional feedback loop is essential for sustaining our action, as emotional states are not static. Spending too long in one can lead to depression on the one hand and naïve optimism on the other. The dynamic movement between the two is fundamental for movement building. While I'm in despair, someone else's momentum has moved them to hope, and vice versa. When you're in despair, you don't need to be taking action. In fact, knowing that someone else somewhere in the world is in hope, offers you permission to take a moment and exist in the feeling first and foremost. So, what if saying yes to despair is not the erasure of hope, but the chrysalis for it?

My friend Jamie Bristow once said to me, "People can't decide whether changemaking is a marathon, or a sprint. But really it's neither, it's a relay race." What he meant was that we are passing the baton to one another from year to year and generation to generation. It's a race of unknown length and unlimited participants, meaning that the burden is not yours alone to carry. This has stayed with me, giving me more permission to feel how I feel, knowing that I'm not dropping the baton, I'm passing it. And in passing it and sitting at my own banquet, I am doing the work of resilience.

Nowadays, when Despair wants to eat a little more at the banquet, I stop, observe and enquire. Firstly, I take a breath or sit still for a moment. Next, I observe, non-judgementally and see who is sitting at my Council today. Finally, I enquire, "Hello Despair, enjoy the food, what do you have to say today?" On hearing what Despair replies, I respond with non-judgement and compassion. "You need ice cream for breakfast? Okay, let me get you a spoon."

Gardening Our Minds: Emotional Permaculture

Permaculture is an agricultural design philosophy rooted in working *with* nature rather than against it, to create sustainable and self-sufficient food and land systems. Permaculture insists that we observe and interact with the environment before making changes and that valuing diversity in crops creates resilience. It also champions creatively responding to change rather than resisting it. *Emotional* permaculture takes these principles and applies them to our emotional landscapes.

Emotional permaculture is the practice of gardening our minds, working with emotions rather than against them.

It embraces the vast spectrum of human emotions that will be planted in our minds, opting for a diverse ecosystem rather than monocultures of hopelessness or optimism. By observing or softening to what is, through mindfulness, introspection or peer support (Guideposts 1 and 2), we are able to respond creatively rather than impulsively. In this way we build a strong and sustainable inner garden.

Near the halfway point of our eight-week model, we invite circles to host a Climate Café to practise tending to our inner gardens. A Climate Café is an emotionally informed conversation about the climate. Held in groups of strangers, it encourages unstructured open dialogue, deep listening and community-building. Participants are invited to speak openly about how they feel about the climate crisis, to begin the process of sitting with and befriending difficult emotions. Popularized by the Climate Psychology Alliance, they advocate for the therapeutic benefit of facing difficult truths – another variation on "fight the dragon, get the gold".

While Climate Cafés can be powerful, at The Resilience Project we recognized additional needs from our youth network for community-building and joy. That's why we developed People, Planet, Picnic, a variation on the Climate I model, with a focus on community-building, decompression and sustenance. We train young people to hold People, Planet, Picnics where other youth can bring and share food, and they've been held in more than 15 countries to date. Looking directly at the climate emergency can sometimes feel too confronting, but doing so with passive activities like eating can make difficult conversations easier. Starting with food rather than climate means starting with connection, nourishment, replenishment and energy. Food is also a connection to the planet we are working so hard to save. Considering our dinner plates and all the hands that worked to make a meal possible can not only deepen our gratitude (an essential balance to work that is often harrowing or heartbreaking) but can offer insight into the interconnectedness of global systems. The following exercise invites you to host your People, Planet, Picnic.

EXERCISE: HOSTING A PEOPLE, PLANET, PICNIC – SHARING AND DEEP LISTENING

Objective: A People, Planet, Picnic is a community-led event, where you can invite others to bring and share food while having open conversations about the permacrisis. There's no fixing, no judging, just open sharing and connection. If you'd like to host your own, you can find more information at www.theresilienceproject.org.uk

Materials needed:

- A quiet, comfortable space
- A timer (phone, watch or clock)
- Optional: tea, snacks or a symbolic object (e.g. a stone or talking stick) to pass when speaking
- Optional: a notebook each for post-exercise reflections

Step 1: Welcome (10–15 minutes)

- Greet participants warmly and introduce yourself.
- Welcome all emotions into the space, naming nerves, excitement, scepticism, hope.
- Explain what the Climate Café model and emotional permaculture are, reading from the above paragraph in the book.

- State that this is a space to talk about the many shades and complexities of how we *feel* about the world without judgement, rather than a space to debate perspectives, news or feel pressure to take action.
- Establish ground rules:
  - Respect and confidentiality (what's shared in the Picnic stays in the Picnic).
  - No judgement (there's no right or wrong way to feel).
  - Everyone gets a chance to speak (but it's okay to just listen).
  - Boundaries (don't unpack anything you don't feel you can safely repack afterwards).

Step 2: Icebreaker Activity (10–15 minutes, optional)

- Example: One Word Check-in or our favourite Resilience Project question: What's your favourite type of potato? (Chips, waffles, mash etc.)

Step 3: Open Discussion (40–60 minutes)

- Let the conversation flow naturally, but have a few conversation prompts ready if needed:
  - What emotions come up when you think about the world?
  - Have you had a moment where you felt hopeful or hopeless about the future?
  - How do your perspectives on the world affect your daily life or your future plans?
  - Where do you find hope and resilience?
- As a facilitator, listen actively. You don't need to respond to each share. Let the dialogue flow between the participants but do contribute your own thoughts and encourage voices who haven't spoken. Avoid dominating the conversation.

Step 4: Closing Reflection (10–15 minutes)

- Ask participants how it felt to share openly.
- Encourage people to connect beyond the session.
- Plan a joyful activity afterwards, from a group song to going to the cinema together.

Final Tips

- Keep it informal and welcoming – this isn't a lecture, it's a shared experience.
- Don't force action – this is about emotional connection, not problem-solving.
- Be flexible – let the conversation flow naturally, silence is fine and natural!
- Encourage joy – discussing climate emotions can be heavy, so consider joyful activities to finish.

CHAPTER 8: GUIDEPOST 4 – NARRATIVES: RESIST, RECLAIM AND REIMAGINE

"You have to act as if it were possible to radically transform the world. And you have to do it all the time." [36]

Angela Davis

Narratives are the stories we tell ourselves about each other, ourselves and our societies. They shape our understanding of the world and our place in it. Metanarratives such as capitalism and patriarchy are overarching, societal-level stories or frameworks that provide a broad explanation for how the world functions and why. They shape cultural, political and economic systems by offering guiding principles and values, influencing the way we view our roles in society. Narratives such as "Your job equals your social status", "We work a five-day week and have a two-day weekend", and "Boys don't wear pink", have become deeply ingrained in cultural norms and practices. But these stories are exactly that: stories. They are narratives masquerading as truth, and hence there is space for resistance, reclamation and reimagination.

Capitalist metanarratives contribute to burnout as the tenets of perpetual growth, competition and efficiency insinuate that we must constantly do more to be of value. In this context, individual contributions to changemaking are often framed as never enough; there is always more that could be done, a higher level of sacrifice to be achieved. This pressure can transform a genuine desire to help into an exhausting burden. Burnout becomes not an unfortunate by-product, but a predictable consequence of internalizing the capitalist ideal that our worth is measured by how much we can produce, give or sacrifice, regardless of the cost to ourselves.

Layered atop this is the influence of another metanarrative of white supremacy, which has long dictated whose labour is valued, whose voices are heard and whose lives are considered worthy of saving. White supremacy constructs spoken and unspoken hierarchies of worthiness, even within movements for justice and sustainability. It has historically privileged some voices as experts while dismissing, exploiting, oppressing or tokenizing People of Colour and LGBTQIA+ folk. White supremacy, at its core, is a system of power and control that establishes and maintains a social hierarchy where whiteness is held as the standard of value, intelligence and morality. The notion of perfectionism, deeply embedded in white supremacy, dictates that there is a right way to be, act and succeed, which is an impossible, often rigidly defined ideal that few can attain. Historically it has imposed stringent, often unattainable, expectations upon marginalized communities, demanding they "prove" their worthiness, capability or humanity in ways that are never required of those who hold privilege, meaning they need to work twice as hard as their privileged counterparts.

Emmanuella Blake Morsi is a young multidisciplinary artist and creative researcher. As a changemaker, they have a passion for reimagining and building opportunities toward a more inclusive and meaningful world. For all the amazing work they have contributed, they are no stranger to burnout. They shared with me how metanarratives have shaped their life: "I was born in Port Harcourt, Nigeria and grew up in Bristol, UK being a Black, Queer, neurodiverse migrant. I had so much internalized hatred that was fixed around misogynoir, which has racism and sexism intertwined. You're raised to believe that you're not good enough and you have to achieve so much more to prove your value. It led to a lot of misplaced hurt and pain where you're conditioned to feel disempowered, and becoming frequently depressed, suicidal and unwell. As I got older and evolved in my self-awareness, internal work and outer activism, it's been such a powerful thing to learn that my burnout has been a lot more intrinsically related to not being able to function in the current state of society that normalizes capitalism, white supremacy and ableism."

Emmanuella continues, "We've built society in a way that your ability to function requires constant output, lacks space for reflection and sees difference and empathy as weakness. So, we don't start with the tools or infrastructure we need to build systems of care. There are many barriers to building progressive solutions that address the harms that have already been done, let alone offer an alternative way of doing and being. So, it's essential on this journey we counter these narratives and understand the importance of our role as part of wider action within communities, as this becomes vital for redistribution of resources and more focused contributions, which nurtures long-term resilience in this work."

Emmanuella speaks to the heart of this work: the narratives inherited by Western society and traditional education structures do not offer us the tools to collectively thrive and flourish. Internal work, collective healing and rewriting narratives become of critical importance, or we will further create spaces that mirror unequal, unfair and individualistic systems. Interrogating the stories we've been told unearths the rich landscape of things we might need to unlearn.

While metanarratives can be likened to the play we have found ourselves cast in, personal, social and community narratives can be likened to the script we've been given.

These are culturally shared stories that shape collective identities and aspirations, often providing a sense of purpose or direction and influencing our perceptions of success and failure. In my own youth activist space, I saw narratives crafting a collective idea of what it means to be an effective activist, leading to burnout, exhaustion and self-sacrifice. For example, the narrative that "You need to be a perfect activist" was never uttered, but it was collectively felt, inherited from broader, more historic structures. Perfect activism looked like being clued up on every socio-environmental issue, making no mistakes with terminology, being meticulously vegan, and living as close to a zero-carbon lifestyle as possible. Baked into this narrative was another: you're not worthy if you're not perfect. If someone deviated from this impossible standard, they were shamed or seen as less committed. We internalized the belief that if we fell short of perfect, we were no use. We were an imposter. We did not belong.

Striving for perfection manifests in the constant, exhausting drive to "do it all", to make no errors and never to appear inconsistent. This false ideal reinforces hierarchies within movements, favouring those with the time and capacity to appear more productive. It creates exclusionary dynamics that undermine solidarity and community, causing some youth to not only leave the movement but feel damaged by it. Those who are perceived to fall short, whether through lack of expertise, resources, or even by making honest mistakes, are often dismissed, shamed or sidelined, mirroring the systemic marginalization baked into white supremacy itself. The constant need to showcase achievements, accumulate knowledge or demonstrate one's commitment through tangible acts results in a culture that prioritizes optics over genuine impact. Conflict becomes the main reason for quitting – not because of climate politics but because of human politics.

EXERCISE: UNEARTHING NARRATIVES

Objective: Consider the non-exhaustive list of narratives below that I've come across in changemaking spaces that I've heard over the years. Then write down reflections about the questions that follow, making a list of all the examples you have experienced.

Harmful narratives contribute to our feelings of burnout as we feel stress, pressure and inadequacy at collective, individual and systemic levels. Try to speak using "I", citing your own experiences rather what you imagine others feel. Remember that narratives are different for all of us.

Narratives

- To be a legitimate changemaker, I must live a completely eco-compliant life.
- I'm not doing enough.
- It's my responsibility to fix this.
- If I don't do it, who will?
- My actions won't make a difference.
- Because of the horrors that are unfolding, rest is self-indulgent.
- Taking time off is selfish.
- Really looking at these crises will inhibit my productivity, so I can't.
- The urgency of the crisis means that I need to give my whole self to the cause.

Questions

- Which narratives above did you resonate with? When do you feel them more and less intensely?

- What narratives contribute to feelings of exhaustion for you? If you're at the beginning of your changemaking journey, have a think about what leads to exhaustion in your personal life.
- Using examples from your own experience, what narratives fuel burnout in changemaking spaces (online and offline)?

Resist, Reclaim, Reimagine and Re-emerge

Identifying the narratives that shape our actions and beliefs is the first step in resisting them, reclaiming their power and reimagining them for the better. Resisting narratives that feel harmful to ourselves, our wellbeing and our work is what I term "flipping the script". For example:

- Resist individualism by building spaces for collective care, or third spaces.
- Resist the narrative that rest is lazy by declining the pull for constant productivity.
- Resist "the movement needs me now" with "the movement needs me healthy, well and at full capacity".
- Resist "perfection" by embracing "progress".

Nobody can live a perfect life in an imperfect system. I have spent countless hours agonizing over small decisions I've made. Even this year, I declined an invitation to my brother's baby shower as I'd have to get on a plane. I wanted to retain my goodness; I was doing this for his baby's future. So, it was a surprise when he started swerving my calls, finally sharing over the phone that he felt deeply hurt, like he wasn't a priority. Through tears, I booked the flight, feeling the shame that I'd not only let my movement down but scuppered my familial relationships in the process.

While I've been working on correcting my narratives for years, they still run deep in my psyche. Unlearning is a long process that requires perpetual grace. My new narrative is "progress, not perfection". This doesn't weaken my approach; it offers me permission to defy my own unattainable standards. The above is a tricky example to give, because ideals can certainly be met – I didn't *need* to get that flight – but it might have come at the expense of my relationships, a great fuel source. By rewriting unrealistic ideals, we free ourselves to take imperfect but impactful actions without fear of being judged or discredited, even if that judgement is coming from ourselves.

We can also reclaim narratives that have been created to minimize our power. A great example of this is the reclamation of the word "dyke". Once used as a slur to degrade and marginalize lesbians, it is being adopted by many lesbian campaigners as a badge of pride, resistance and identity. My own personal favourite reclamation is the term "snowflake", describing a liberal left-wing tendency for sensitivity, suggesting that when we are touched, we melt. We are easily triggered. But en masse, the only thing snowflakes trigger are avalanches. Their collective form is one of power, uprooting and repaving. I embrace my sensitivity and find the power in being one small part of this enormous avalanche of change.

When we resist, reclaim and reimagine better narratives, we re-emerge with a different sense of what meaningful action looks like, detached from the drive to do and be it all. How we show up matters. Modelling narratives shifts how we re-enter changemaking spaces. Impact isn't a perfectly crafted new narrative, but how we walk the talk in embodying its essence in all aspects of life. The opportunity is not just to bring these narratives as discussion points to your groups, friends and family relationships, but also to practise and integrate them. For example, what would it feel like to douse voices of jealousy or insecurity with the narrative "comparison is the thief of joy"? You might actively celebrate others with more ease or feel a pull to text something you appreciate about them to someone you're struggling with. You might start to develop partnerships with other groups rather than fearing competition, and co-design an awesome campaign. Re-emergence leads to increased connection with others and self, but importantly it's the groundwork for solidarity and cooperation within our work. Outside of changemaking, how would your life be impacted if you reframed your pain? As actress Keke Palmer quipped about an ex, "You did not break up with me, you released me." *I wasn't rejected from the job, I was redirected to something else. I didn't embarrass myself in front of my ex, I displayed all of my gorgeous humanity.*

Resisting and reimagining narratives takes consistent work. For example, the relentless push for "more" does not stem solely from within. It is deeply entrenched in a culture that seeks to exploit both people and the planet. These are ideas we've seen in films, read in books and heard in anecdotes and obituaries. Impact is resisting the pull to overwork, modelling new ways of being *and* also challenging the systems that created the narrative in the first place. True change is born from dismantling the structures that dehumanize us all.

Flip the Script

Flipping the script involves identifying narratives that can be damaging to ourselves, our relationships and our campaign work and reimagining an alternative. For example, if you carry the narrative "I'm not doing enough", you can begin to challenge this by acknowledging and appreciating the actions you have taken, however small they may seem. By doing so, you create a new story: "Every effort I make contributes to the larger movement." The table on page 112 is filled with examples taken from youth groups I've worked with on this exercise. You can copy the table into your journal to complete your own.

We also need to explore: "What do we open up and close when we flip the script?" This is because life is full of nuance. In changing the story, we might also be shutting down other important functions of a narrative. For example, cancel culture or "calling someone out" involves public shaming and stunting meaningful dialogue. Instead, "calling someone in" involves privately bringing someone into a conversation when they may have intentionally or unintentionally caused harm. The latter is more likely to lead to change, as it removes the heightened shame tactics that typically create tension and retreat. However, in changing the story, we close the space to promote public dialogue. Some things need to be called out – for example, when a public figure shares something that incites violence. We can't reach them privately anyway, and public sharing offers an important educational moment to others. There is nuance. Another example is "I'm not doing enough". There might be some validity in this. You potentially could be doing more. So, our investigation is one of honest discernment. To aid this, consider if the narrative is coming from shame or encouragement. Shame is not a sustainable force, but encouragement is. Encouragement looks like: "I can use my gifts to offer X amount of time per week. I have something to contribute. Doing more will serve me and others."

EXERCISE: FLIP THE SCRIPT

Objective: To identify and change narratives that are potentially damaging to us.

Consider the narratives and alternatives below and write down some of your own in your journal.

Current narrative	Suggestion for new narrative
Perfection is possible.	The perfect changemaker doesn't exist.
Vulnerability is a weakness.	Vulnerability is a strength.
I'm not doing enough.	I'm trying my best. *Or* I can do more in a way that serves me and others.
If you haven't been arrested, then you're less of an activist.	We all have a role to play in the activism ecosystem. There is no hierarchy of offerings.
This problem is bigger than me. My problems are irrelevant.	I am worthy of good mental health.
Rest is a luxury. Rest is additional to engagement.	Rest is essential. Rest is central to engagement.
The urgency of the climate crisis means we must live perfect low-carbon lives.	There is no such thing as a perfect changemaker. We strive for progress rather than perfection.
Eco-anxiety is a mental health problem that you should try to treat and fix.	Eco-anxiety is a rational response to an emergency.
Feeling tough emotions inhibits action.	Befriending tough emotions is a necessary step to agency and action.
Feeling bad needs to be fixed.	It's okay not to feel okay.

Current narrative	Suggestion for new narrative
If I step back, nothing will get done.	Stepping back when I need to will benefit my activism in the long run and allow others to step forward.
Direct action is the most important form of activism.	Change comes in many shapes and sizes.
I am an activist.	Activism is one part of my identity.
Call people out.	Call people in.
Other people's lives on social media are better/funnier/happier.	Comparison is the thief of joy.

EXERCISE: FINDING THE NUANCE

Objective: What space do we open up, and close, when we flip the script?

Discussion: In pairs, small groups or individually, run through your narrative changes and explore the above question. What opportunities present themselves when we flip the script? Similarly, explore what might be at stake.

CHAPTER 9: GUIDEPOST 5 – THE WISDOM OF BURNOUT

"Caring for myself is not self-indulgence, it is self-preservation, and that is an act of political warfare."[37]

Audre Lorde

Why do we burn out? It's not because we're incapable. It's not because we're weak. It's not because we care too much about the cause. It's not because you didn't do the "ten things successful people do before 5am". It's not because you don't take ice baths. Burnout can be seasonal, unpredictable and compounded. It happens due to systemic factors, narratives which influence how we relate to ourselves and the world, our relationship to work and stress and, importantly, because changemaking is very hard. You're working against unjust and unequal systems that are buttressed by centuries of power. To stand for change is to embrace the loneliness of caring, of being on the smaller, less-resourced side. And all while battling narratives that glorify overwork and overcommitment. In vocations where you are trying to change the system, and go against the grain, burnout can be an occupational hazard. Of course it can.

To stand in the Arena is to accept that you will move in constant *proximity* to burnout. This does *not* mean that you will reach the point of burning out. Counterintuitively, instead of denying burnout, building a constant dialogue to understand where you are in relation to it, is the method of prevention. If burnout is not in your orbit at all, perhaps you have the capacity to engage in bigger, bolder action. If burnout feels close enough to make itself feel felt, then rest, reset and repeat. The sooner we accept this, the sooner we can unlock the true secret to making change without burning out – being less concerned with how to avoid burnout completely and more focused on how we feel stronger, more connected, better resourced and more alive.

Unlock the true secret to making change without burning out.

Stress in Changemakers

Burnout is defined as chronic physical, mental or emotional exhaustion caused by excessive or prolonged stress. It looks and feels different for each of us, because it's relational to stress exposure and management. "Excessive" and "prolonged" are important descriptions here because life is full of stress – from the overstimulation of city living, to questioning if we've overshared on Instagram. The inevitability of stress is up there with death and taxes. That's the gig of being a human. We run into problems when stress becomes excessive (it overwhelms our capacity for management) or it is prolonged (it is sustained for long periods, from months to years, without adequate rest).

Not all stress is created equal. In fact, there are two types, positive (eustress) and negative (distress) with each having different effects on an individual's emotional, mental and physical state. Eustress is a healthy, motivating form of stress that can enhance performance and focus. I think back to the times when I was on the final lap of *Mario Kart*, on the edge of my seat, shoulders up to my ears, using all that "fight" energy to make sure the worst didn't happen – that my brother won yet again. You may imagine your own feelings of eustress – when you're in a timed exam and your brain is firing on all cylinders or you're developing a climate strategy with your group and you can feel a sense of zest and buzz. Eustress is a nifty tool. It can enable creativity and productivity. It can drive effort and growth.

Negative stress, or distress, occurs when stressors become overwhelming and exceed an individual's coping capacity. It leads to feelings of anxiety, helplessness or frustration, often diminishing our performance and allowing our inner critic to thrive. It can have physical consequences like headaches, insomnia or weakened immunity. Unlike eustress, distress detracts from an individual's ability to function effectively. The main difference lies in the outcome: eustress energizes and enhances performance, while distress drains and impairs it.

The distinction is important because distress is easier to spot than eustress, but both contribute to burnout. The body doesn't differentiate between positive and negative cortisol; it releases cortisol irrespectively. So, eustress can still contribute to burnout if it becomes prolonged, excessive or poorly managed. In setting up The Resilience Project, I've had many perplexing moments when I've started to show the early signs of burnout but couldn't make sense of it due to my hyper-productivity and a genuine enjoyment of what I was doing. But imagine living your life in a state as if you were constantly on the final lap of *Mario Kart*, where chaos and drive reign supreme. While this would initially feel energizing and motivating, even positive challenges begin to take a toll when you persist in doing them without adequate recovery or balance. Whereas distress can often be instantly recognized, eustress hides in plain sight.

Both types of stress are especially relevant to changemakers for a whole host of reasons. Firstly, let's talk about our boundary and overcommitment issues. Passion for a chosen cause or goal frequently leads to overextending, blurring the lines between healthy motivation and harmful overwork. Harmful overwork is often justified as the morally correct decision, particularly when both the urgency of crises and the small size of the movement means that we feel we need to do enough work for ten times the amount of people. Secondly, eustress often accompanies high aspirations or goals, such as policy wins or entire systemic change. If these goals are not met, the resulting disappointment can erode motivation and move us into distress. Thirdly, in the case of these enormous social justice issues like climate change or the refugee crisis, they aren't going to be fixed overnight. Stress becomes a journey of unknown distance. We may find ourselves consistently taking on demanding but rewarding tasks without periods of rest, creating a cumulative and multiplying stress effect. The phrase "I will rest when…" is a common example of delaying our resilience. In an age of crisis after crisis, "when" seemingly never comes. Finally, excitement and focus driven by eustress can sometimes overshadow basic needs like sleep, nutrition and relaxation – for example, at COP (the international climate negotiations), where you exist in an enormous space with no windows for two weeks straight, fuelled only by eustress and coffee. This is one of the reasons why COP is considered an energetic tent pole moment, where your energy spikes to a peak in the lead-up and during, and crashes afterwards, mirroring the image of a tent.

While stress is generated in our own bodies, it can feel like an external force. A valid critique of the resilience movement is: "My sector/organization/group needs reform, I don't need to become more 'resilient.'" There is some truth in this, your sector undoubtably does need reform. Blaming burnout on the individual and putting the emphasis on them to adapt is a convenient way to deflect scrutiny from deeply ingrained group dynamics, power asymmetries or organizational working cultures (and save time and money). But equally, blaming the system and culture in totality is a convenient way for us not to do the work. There is a both/and here. Inner work shouldn't shift our gaze away from systems and structures, the two should work hand in hand. For example, developing your own sense of empathy and calm could lead to meaningful and constructive dialogue in your group or organization – I know from my own experience that difficult conversations are enabled more by how we regulate our nervous system than the facts and figures we're presenting. Sharing your sector struggles through peer support may compel you to write a blog to illuminate burnout cultures and build a collective mandate for change. Reconciling with your own patterns of "people-pleasing" might develop your ability to set clear boundaries. Categorically, no sector or structure should be excused through disproportionate focus on the individual. Equally, I'm yet to meet someone – myself and my cat included – that isn't also a work in progress.

Burnout: Signs and Symptoms

From the many stories I've heard as well as my own experience, burnout in changemakers looks different to the signs and symptoms you'll see online. Some of the symptoms I've come across include, but are not limited to:

- High performance, low satisfaction
- Persistent feelings of exhaustion, even after rest
- Apathy and feelings of "What's the point?"
- Disillusionment with the cause or with the movement entirely
- Feeling so heavy and weighed down that that you feel pinned to your bed
- A declining sense of impact
- Nervous system dysregulation, including panic/anxiety attacks
- Detachment from responsibilities, campaigners or colleagues
- Sleep disturbances, including insomnia or restless sleep
- Weakened immune system and increased susceptibility to illnesses

- Increased irritability, impatience or frustration
- Reliance on food, medication, alcohol or drugs to cope with stress
- Feeling overwhelmed by seemingly small tasks
- Feeling a sense of dread at WhatsApp notifications or emails
- Not replying for days and weeks
- Declining social engagements and shrinking your social circles
- Feeling like you're constantly letting people down
- Feelings of "freeze" in response to news stories
- Feeling insecure
- Reduced appetite for showering or personal hygiene
- Unkind thoughts
- Emotional disregularity
- Crying a lot
- General feelings of being unhinged or untethered

RHIANNON'S STORY: SYSTEMS AND BURNOUT

Burnout can happen to anyone, anywhere, at any time. However, it's crucial to recognize that burnout is deeply systemic. Some start life with predetermined stressors. Already illuminated in Emmanuella's story in Chapter 8, systemic burnout is related to who we are and how valued we are by the pervasive systems (capitalism, patriarchy and white supremacy being the three largest). It relates to our complex identities and our class, race, gender presentation, genetics, ability and sexuality to name just a few.

I spoke to Rhiannon Hawkins, who I trained to run a Resilience Circle in 2024. She is a disabled and autistic climate activist, 24 years old and is now completing her PhD at the University of Glasgow. Rhiannon shared:

"Burnout for me is a constant. I think disabled people will constantly feel burned out to some extent. It never goes away for our community, because we have to constantly advocate for our own rights and our own challenges and our own existence within space, because of how our society has been built. It just isn't made for us. It's not made for me.

"My mum constantly had to advocate for me and that made me exhausted because I felt like I was a burden on her. You grow up thinking that you're not suited to this environment, and it's a problem. That you're a problem. So, you exhaust yourself constantly as you think, 'I am a burden' because I'm having to have other people carrying me constantly.

"At university I had to fight for 50 per cent extra time in my exams, even though I was entitled to this by my diagnosis under the Equality Act of 2010, and to be protected. Now in my PhD, I'm still having to constantly explain myself and my needs, and they are often not acknowledged. It's absolutely exhausting. I'm realizing that it's like pulling up a mountain, because it builds up and up and up and up over and over and over and over consecutively. And then you feel as if you have the whole world on your head, and sometimes just don't want to get out of bed and deal with it that day."

Resilience Not Resignation

Rhiannon's story highlights the additional stressors on people who our society has not been built for or shaped by. She is fierce in her resolve to improve life for both herself and others. While burnout is systemic, we all still have agency to better resource and strengthen ourselves. With reference to internal activation, she reflects:

"Going through the eight-week steps has helped me realize that I've got to pace myself. I've got to prioritize myself a bit more. I, as an individual, am worth something. The movement will constantly take from you, but you have to understand your own needs and yourself first, because even if the movement 'needs' you, there will always be a time when you can go back in and out of it, and I've learned not to be so 'I have to do everything in the movement.' Because the movement is not your life. It's not going to go away if you step back. It's going to reform itself multiple, multiple times. We've seen that over the past ten years, when the climate movement has changed its ways of activism and campaigning. It's changed its ways of navigating the current political system. The disability movement is the same. We've changed and morphed multiple, multiple times over the generations. There's always been a movement. As early as the 1880s there was a disability movement, and we've continued it."

Burnout Prevention: Self- and Embodied Awareness

If our concern is not avoiding burnout completely but our relative distance from it, then developing our ability to sense where we are in relation to burnout most of the time becomes a key tool in prevention. The eight-week model has been designed to create supportive communities to develop this self-awareness, be that through asking "How are you?" in peer support spaces, understanding what each emotion needs to be a guest in our home or uncovering the narratives that lead to overwork. Any supported strategy that brings us closely to the truth of who and how we are is a form of burnout prevention.

Crucial to this is embodied awareness: the ability to bypass the mind and listen to your body. Under excessive and prolonged stress, it won't be your mental will that gives in first but your body. Burnout taught me that the body is the most reliable narrator. While my mind has been programmed for productivity, focus and logic, the body – the soft and complex labyrinth Life wanders through – has a working memory of all the footprints left within in. The body is the early warning signs in your car. It is the furrowed brow on your mother's face. The body is the keeper of truth. Its pragmatic functions are immune to ego, so it will get hungry when it runs out of sustenance. It will sleep when it needs to recharge. Or it will shut down. The mind on the other hand is a trickster, dictating how far we will go and when we will stop, depending on a lifetime of voices it's heard. It holds the gavel and attempts to decide our sentence – I am burned out. I need to stop. Or, I am not burned out, I'll be fine next week – by assessing what we believe to be evidence. But burnout and breakdown don't bend to the whims of logic and reason. I spent so much energy trying to convince myself that I was not burned out and there was not enough available evidence for someone like me, with the privilege I have, to be burned out. In doing so, I was not listening to the whispers of my body, softening to what *is*. If I'd have paid it more notice, I would not have ended up so beaten, bruised and broken.

No matter how mentally strong or supported you are, trauma and stress leave their marks on the nervous system. To use myself as an example, starting my own organization has required sustained periods of eustress and distress. Consider meeting tight deadlines, the responsibility of managing a team, the anticipation of hosting residentials and the nerves of pitching to funders. While all of these may range from eustress to distress, they all impact the nervous system by moving it from a parasympathetic state (rest and digest) to an elevated sympathetic state (fight, flight and freeze). The sympathetic state is fundamental for drive, survival and response, but staying in either state for too long can bring consequences. The aim is a regulated nervous system, which moves between the two. For me, since 99 per cent of my work is laptop based, my nervous system would find itself in a state of fight or flight while staring at the screen. This unconscious response became synonymous with laptop work, and I'd find myself tense and stressed on a Sunday morning when looking up recipes for the week. My nervous system would conflate laptop and threat, changing my state as a protection mechanism.

Over the years I have learned that burnout prevention isn't simply about narratives (mind) or rest (body), but also the nervous system, which has been critically overlooked. In times of great stress, my mantras of "I can do this. I can do another big, scary thing", did wonders to overcome the additional pressures of imposter syndrome. But they also overrode the signals of my nervous system, keeping me in fight or flight mode for sustained periods of time. In Chapter 7, I mentioned that I'd started having panic attacks at times when I believed my mind was in check. I didn't notice any narratives of anxiety or inadequacy, and my diet was nourishing and plentiful. I was monitoring my proximity to burnout and felt it was far away. Yet still I found my body unconsciously moving into a state of fight or flight – once on a work call, another time around a table with new friends and again when I was quietly watching a documentary the week after a very intense and fantastic work trip. My nervous system was on such high alert that it perceived threat all around, be that the judgement of new friends, the reminder of work or the moment of stillness after a huge adrenaline surge.

Though the panic attacks were distressing, and I questioned if I was broken, the experience illuminated the nervous system as an area to explore. Resilience and mindfulness often cite the trio of mind, body and soul/spirit. They are three touch points to consider during times of deflation or feeling stuck. We can consider any deficiencies in our physical body, any saboteurs in our minds or how to nourish and expand our spirit. The nervous system has something to offer too. In periods of stress, go beyond an analysis of what your mind or body need, and consider: what does *my nervous system* need? What do you do to regulate your own nervous system? For me, regulating my nervous system looks like actively rejecting busyness and finding places to let go. I don't find it in sitting meditation, as I'm still on high alert, but I do find it in slow, mindful walking, in saunas and in locking my bedroom door for 20 minutes, lying under my duvet and finding a yoga nidra, a guided form of meditation that is considered to be a massage for your nervous system. I find it in genuine stillness.

Stillness is the mind's foe but the body's ally. We know this by how we desperately grab for our phone when something is taking too long to load on our computer, or how we mindlessly scroll through reels in between daily activities. Finding moments in your day or week for stillness is an offering for the body and the nervous system. This doesn't need to be the stillness of lying down (physical rest) or an eight-day retreat. But it should be stillness without phones, unmindful movement or watching TV. It could be slowly drinking your coffee in the morning, feeling the warmth in your hands, taking a five-minute movement break at work/uni, yoga or any form of stillness that gives us a moment to connect the mind to the body and the nervous system within it. It can simply be ten minutes at the end of the day, before sleep, to think, "What stories and narratives have run through my mind today?" and, "What's going on in my body?"

Stillness is the mind's foe but the body's ally.

One of the most helpful tools I've found to unlock this embodied awareness is the stress signature, where you identify your stress signs and symptoms. I have copied my example below. Complete your own separately.

Stress Signature	**Warning signs**	**Symptoms**	**What helps is . . .**
Feeling	When I'm stressed, I can feel initial feelings of elation, mania and hyper-productivity. I feel strong, powerful and capable.	Struggling to emotionally regulate; feeling up and down, from laughing to intolerant.	Softening to what is; understanding which emotions are sat at the Banquet; and listening. Let the mind quieten and listen to the body.
Thinking	Sometimes I have a voracious "can-do" attitude, often thinking, "Wow, I can't believe I'm holding this all so well!" followed by deep immediate fatigue. Other times I feel overwhelmed and think, "I can't do this."	Can't sit still and need to be busy. Or can't move, spending more time in bed or lying on the sofa.	Repeating a mantra to invite my nervous system, "You are safe. Stand down. We are good". Self-compassion, non-judgement and permission to do nothing.
Body	At times of stress my body moves into fight, flight and freeze.	Jaw clenching, tense shoulders, fatigue, insomnia, digestive issues, craving comfort foods and carbohydrates.	Getting into the body with yoga, running or the gym. Restorative yoga and gentle walking. Lying on my bed listening to the rain to downregulate my nervous system.

Stress Signature	**Warning signs**	**Symptoms**	**What helps is . . .**
Behaviour	My behaviour often becomes very rigid. I feel like I must be completely on top of my to-do list, and I struggle to rest.	Irritability, mood swings, lack of boundaries around "on" and "off" time, struggling to switch off.	Assessing if first I have my basics covered: am I fed and watered? Have I slept? If yes, reinstating boundaries and finding space for the things I love to do.
Relationships	A tendency for isolation and lashing out at those I love. I can lack functioning judgement capabilities, thinking, "They are the problem because they did X. It's not that I'm stressed."	Mood swings, reduced tolerance and empathy.	Calling my friends and telling people I'm struggling. Asking for more support and allowing myself to be looked after. Baking apology cakes.

Stress Signature	**Warning signs**	**Symptoms**	**What helps is . . .**
Feeling			
Thinking			
Body			
Behaviour			
Relationships			

Another awareness building method is the Yerkes–Dodson Law. The below figure (Figure 2) demonstrates that there is an optimal level of arousal or stress that enhances performance, typically depicted as an inverted U-shaped curve.

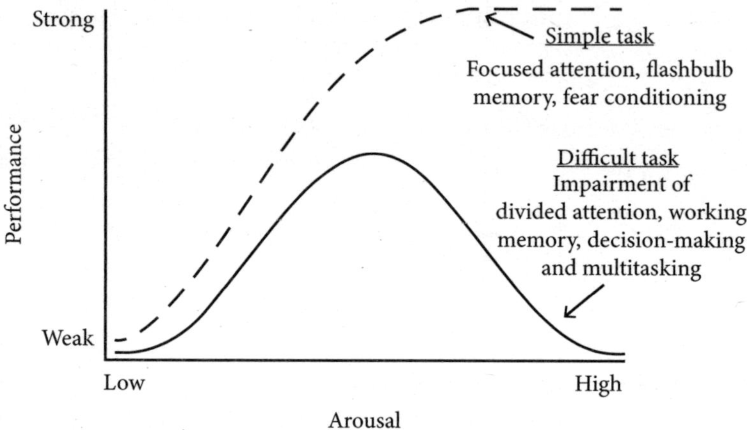

Figure 2: Yerkes–Dodson Law performance–arousal relationship. Data from Yerkes & Dodson (1908). CC0 Public Domain, Wikimedia Commons.[38]

When stress is too low, performance may suffer due to lack of motivation or focus. There may be boredom or a lack of exercise. At moderate levels, stress can enhance concentration and efficiency. However, when stress becomes excessive, we move beyond optimal arousal and performance declines sharply. In this high-arousal range we may exhibit symptoms like fatigue, irritability and inefficiency, the key precursors to burnout and breakdown; at extreme levels we might feel panic, anxiety and collapse. Take a look at the Yerkes–Dodson model (Figure 2) and think through where you are in your journey right now.

Another helpful tool to understand stress is to think of it like a bucket (Figure 3). When life is balanced, stressors flow into the bucket and are processed effectively through the taps (stress release), without overwhelming the individual. Stress flows are different in size. Small inflows could be too much responsibility in your campaign, university deadlines or feeling unable to call something out in your activist setting. Larger inflows could be losing your job, financial difficulties or abusive relationships. The size of our bucket and its ability to hold stress is affected by a host of environmental and social conditions, including our relative levels of systemic power and our genetics.

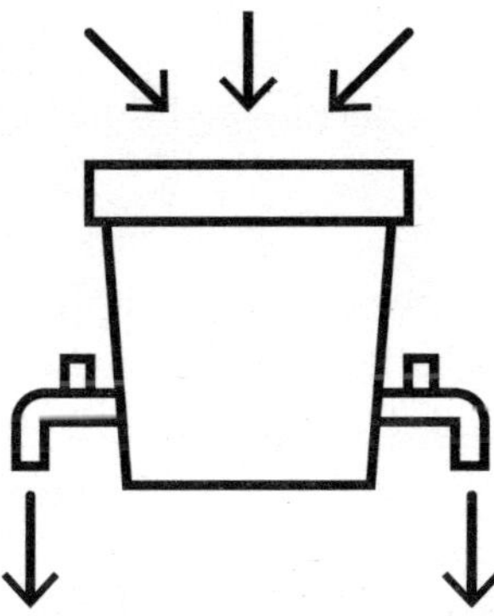

Figure 3: The stress bucket model: stressors fill the bucket and healthy coping strategies act as taps to relieve pressure.

If additional stressors continue to flow into the bucket without relief, due to unresolved issues, poor coping mechanisms or a lack of support, the bucket begins to fill. Eventually, the bucket can overflow, representing a point of crisis where we can no longer manage the accumulated stress. In applying the stress bucket to our own lives, we can identify our inflows – all the things that add stress, both positive and negative – and our taps, which allow us to release stressors from the bucket to prevent overflow. These taps can be our personal strategies, supportive communities or anything that we feel restores balance.

Remember that changemaking does not exist in a vacuum. If we overidentify with the label "changemaker", we might relegate our personal life as less important, but what happens outside of changemaking is likely to be brought into it. The bucket exercise helps us to see that we may have a lot more stressors that meets the eye. A great starter for investigation is to ask: *What's happening in my life in its entirety? What else is on my plate?*

EXERCISE: THE STRESS BUCKET

Objective: This exercise can help us to understand all the sources of our stress and whether or not we need to identify additional taps.

Step 1: Draw a bucket on a piece of paper, ensuring that it has several taps at the bottom.
Step 2: Identify all of the stressors coming into the bucket, filling it. These could be situational, genetic, environmental or systemic.
Step 3: Identify all of your taps: strategies, people, methods and activities that help to empty the bucket of its contents.
Step 4: Assess if your inflows and outflows are balanced. If there are more stressors than strategies, we run the risk of our stress bucket overflowing in unmanageable ways. What additional taps might you need to add?

Burnout Recovery: the Mental Flu

Even with our best prevention mechanisms at play, we may experience burnout. This differs from fatigue, which can be corrected over a weekend of getting plenty of rest and seeing friends and family. Burnout, on the other hand, feels like stepping over a tipping point – pushing your body into a state of breakdown that no massage, yoga class or weekend of sleep will remedy. There is a great irony that in these states of "collapse", you may be too depleted to lean on resilience strategies. Why is it that when we are at our lowest, we need to summon the courage to reach out to a therapist? Or lack the energy to go for walks, cook healthy food or even to shower. You may be in such a state of dysregulation that you are disconnected from understanding your own needs. In my experience, this becomes a downward negative spiral full of judgement and shame.

Consider when you have the flu. The kind of knock-out flu that keeps you firmly in bed. There are no walks or long afternoons cooking. We're inclined to give ourselves what we need, which is probably physical rest, a spirit of gentleness and films from the early 2000s. The mind permits it and shame takes a back seat as we recognize that we are physically incapacitated. The only thing that becomes important is healing and survival. When burnout creeps in, yield not to the mind, but to the body.

When burnout creeps in, yield not to the mind, but to the body.

I have since reframed burnout, or feeling the first fluttering of burnout, as the "mental flu". Like the physical flu, mental flu is not forever. If physical flu is a natural occurrence each winter, then mental flu may come around seasonally in our own personal winter. It's not a personal failing, but a seasonal occurrence in response to changing conditions. Rather than breaking us, time, rest and acceptance will heal us from the flu. This reframe encourages the mind to quieten and respond through the body. We can't "think" our way out of the mental flu. We must rest. We must sleep. We must be kind to ourselves. Would I go on a run with the physical flu? No. Would I feel the need to be productive? No. Would I berate myself for eating seven bagels in succession? Heck no. So why should it be any different for the mental flu? It's a reframe that removes shame and guilt from the equation and offers full permission to slow down. Saying yes to the mental flu is the first stage of burnout recovery: Ground (see page 133).

The GROWTH Recovery Arc

Burnout recovery is not simply about bringing our body back to stasis. Unlike the physical flu, healing burnout takes longer than a few weeks. There is no course of antibiotics or emergency surgery for this kind of pain. After my first burnout, I didn't step back into changemaking for 12 months. I didn't do any direct organizing for 18 months. Clinically, burnout recovery ranges from several months to more than a year. From hearing personal stories, my assessment is that burnout recovery ranges from a few months to five years. This is why it's so important not to exceed our tipping points and build awareness of our proximity to burnout, because once the threshold is crossed, the damage is done. If you have crossed the threshold of burnout, my first advice is: be generous with your timelines for healing. Physical symptoms may ease quicker, but a heart untended to requires time. Stepping back into places that caused harm too quickly may be accompanied by energetic whiplash, where you feel like you're back to square one. Your nervous system may not have fully recovered and you may find yourself right back in fight, flight or freeze.

There are many stages to recovery, and in fact I identify six: Ground, Recognize, Open, Weave, Thrive and Hold – I call them the GROWTH Recovery Arc. This highlights recovery, which is found beyond rest. True burnout recovery is less about self-care and more about self-change. Beyond restoration or passivity, burnout recovery is how we unlock the wisdom to emerge as someone newly forged, with better boundaries, more vitality and an appreciation of all the energy for life that exists around us.

True burnout recovery is less about self-care and more about self-change.

Step 1: **G** – **Ground** (rest, regulate, recalibrate)
Key statement: The body leads the way.
This is the immediate and necessary withdrawal from activity. It's marked by exhaustion, passivity and the body demanding deep rest. Nervous system down-regulation, sleep and stillness are core. People may feel numb, disconnected or guilty for doing less – which is normal. Try to reframe this is as the mental flu. Resist the urge to think, process or reflect.

Step 2: **R** – **Recognize** (reflect, name patterns, identify root causes)
Key question: How did we get here?
As the body begins to stabilize, we gain the cognitive and emotional space to reflect. This includes identifying patterns, root causes (internal and systemic) and unlearning beliefs like "rest is laziness", or "I am only as worthy as my output." Peer support becomes invaluable in this stage to begin the sense-making process of how we got here.

Step 3: **O** – **Open** (allow healing, self-compassion, vulnerability)
Key question: What needs to heal or shift?
The next stage is opening ourselves up to heal, forgive and change. This phase bridges inner and outer change. We begin tending to wounds, such as betrayal, disillusionment or over-responsibility and gently shift our internal compass. We explore our boundaries, needs and values. Therapy, coaching or somatic work often happens here.

Step 4: **W** — **Weave** (introduce new boundaries, practices, patterns)
Key question: How do I live differently?
Step 4 is connected to renewal. Here, actions return slowly. We begin weaving the wisdom from Reflect and Open into our lives and spaces. We implement the behaviour changes identified earlier: setting boundaries,

saying no, prioritizing joy, rest and balance. This is where new habits, support systems and personal practices are established.

Step 5: **T** — **Thrive** (reconnect with energy, aliveness, purpose)
Key question: What brings me to aliveness?
With a regulated nervous system and revised inner landscape, vitality resurfaces. Curiosity, creativity and purpose start to pulse again. We reconnect with the world not through urgency or obligation, but through joy, community and a sense of wholeness. How do we feel aliveness? We jump in cold water, we cry and laugh with friends, we connect with a sense of awe and wonder, we mindfully travel. We pause to feel the wind, we learn new skills, we reconnect with who we were, we remember that Life is pulsating around us always. We set the alarm early and notice the sunrise, we stay up late and notice the moon, we listen to inspiring podcasts and we do things that give us goosebumps. We live hard and we love harder. We do the work. Vitality is our life force, energy, connection to self and freedom. The antidote to burnout is not rest, it's aliveness.

The antidote to burnout is not rest, it's aliveness.

Step 6: **H** — **Hold** (integrate and sustain wisdom over time)
Key question: How does this change who I am?
This final phase is often overlooked, and it concerns wisdom and integration. It's about metabolizing the experience of burnout and folding the insights into long-term practice. Not self-care, self-change. We emerge not as the old self restored, but as someone newly forged. Moving through the same spaces, here we hold our new self, rooted.

The Gifts of Burnout

It is unlikely that driving change will get easier, particularly in the wake of rampant AI development and a surge of right-wing extremism. We will probably get close to burnout again. We might move through the GROWTH Recovery Arc many times. This is why we Act, Rest, Reset and importantly we Repeat. From my own experience, in one year I can feel righteous when I say no, firm in my worth and by the next season I'm working myself into the ground due to an idea I've latched on to of what "enough" looks like. Without continually engaging with our inner work, we may find ourselves needing to move through the Arc again. Consider the activists on social media who speak about the necessity of rest and then find themselves quite courageously crying into their front camera due to exhaustion. To move back to exhaustion is not to be invalidated or weak. Those activists – and me – are armoured with the experiential knowledge that our emotional states are knitted together by threads of external conditions, metanarratives and narratives that live deep within us. Paired with the notion that all of this and all of us can be visible through social media indefinitely, moving back to exhaustion is understandable. This is why our inner work needs to become a way of life rather than a piece of homework. Learning the fabric of our psyche takes intentional practice; it takes time and crucially it takes a hell of a lot of self-compassion. Each time you move through the Arc you find gifts that will inform how you move through the world in a healthier and kinder way.

Unlearning and relearning is a life-long journey. So, remove the guilt. Adding a layer of "How have I let myself get into this state yet again?" intensifies the emotional picture. While we can't change the exhaustion right this second, we have more agency in liberating ourselves from the shame associated with it; we can soften to what is and ground ourselves.

When burnout arrives, it doesn't ask for shame, it asks for insight. The glorious opportunity here – and I do mean it when I say glorious – is that there is no changemaking journey without a parallel journey in building resilience and learning who we are. Social transformation will call on you to be your biggest and most fearless self. It might feel overwhelming because you're reading this as the person you are, not as the person you're going to become. The response becomes not "I can't do this anymore", but "I can't do this *in this way* anymore. What needs to change?" Not "How do I work harder", but "How do I resource myself better?"

In the case of burnout, it is not building a life that avoids stress and tiredness. If that were the case, you wouldn't be reading this book. Sustainable changemaking is building a life where our relationship with stress and tiredness also creates space for aliveness. One part of me feels deeply tired, yes, but how can other parts of me feel alive?

For a while I thought that burnout happened *to* me. Now I think burnout happened *for* me. I developed a deep love, care and understanding of who I am, and an empathy for others moving through it. I moved from the city to the Scottish Highlands to Thrive and I built deeper community and a deeper sense of my own aliveness. I started to appreciate who I am beyond the fight. For all my inner work, living in a small town in the mountains and my writings on burnout, I am not immune to it. In fact, the process of writing this book, running an international climate organization and the uncontrollable happenings of my personal life have brought me great bouts of deep fatigue. It proved yet another opportunity to reflect on how far I've come, move through the GROWTH Recovery Arc and hunt for the aliveness within me. Burnout doesn't break us, it cracks us open to let in the light.

Burnout doesn't break us, it cracks us open to let in the light.

CHAPTER 10:

GUIDEPOST 6 – YOUR RESILIENCE RUCKSACK

"First forget inspiration. Habit is more dependable. Habit will sustain you whether you're inspired or not."[39]

Octavia Butler

Resilience is not a fixed trait. We aren't born resilient or not. It is something we intentionally unlock, through seismic life events, healing, transformation and intentional work. Even once we've done the inner work, resilience can fluctuate – trust me. You will move through seasons of feeling more able to participate than others, which is why building the *practice* of resilience is fundamental for long-term engagement with your cause. This requires both an understanding of our strategies to unlock resilience and the intention of committing to them regularly. Intentional practice – or resilience strategies – are often overlooked as something we do at the point of crisis rather than something we weave into our life. They can be considered superfluous. I'm here to tell you that they are *not*. Our minds may convince us that intentional and regular practice is not important, because deep down we don't want to engage with the discipline, time and effort that they require. Waking up early to write, read or craft is not easy. Meal planning on a Sunday when you're exhausted is not easy. Getting yourself off social media and out for an evening walk is not easy. But we can do hard things.

In fact, this world requires us to do so. If you can do the hard thing of loving a failing world, you can do the hard thing of positive practice too. You're worth it.

Resilience as a Rucksack

Instead of resilience as a binary concept – you either have it or you don't – imagine instead your sense of resilience like a rucksack. Some days it's light, filled with rest and laughter. Other days it's crammed with sorrow, doubt and the silent weight of trying. But the beauty of the rucksack is that it can be unpacked, repacked and shared every single day. Our resilience rucksack reminds us that resilience isn't an inherent and endless resource but something we carry around with us every day that requires our consistent attention.

The first step is to turn our attention lovingly toward our rucksack and see what heavy things we are holding. These could be a range of stressors: relationship difficulties, work anxiety or simply hanger (hunger-induced anger). We then have the opportunity to repack them – alone or with others – with the things that nourish and sustain us. We refill our rucksacks with the large, medium and small contents that engender our feelings of strength and capacity.

Large items are the foundational elements of resilience, including basics like sufficient sleep, nourishing food and a sense of safety. When these large items are missing from our rucksack, our ability to manage stress and challenge is severely compromised. Medium items include lifestyle practices and activities that can help maintain balance, such as running clubs, meaningful conversations or asking for support from trusted people. Medium items remind us that self-care is not a one-time event but an ongoing commitment. Finally, small items, while seemingly less impactful, can have a surprisingly significant effect during moments of adversity. Simple pleasures like laughter, a good oat flat white or feeling the sun on our skin can lift our spirits and remind us why life is worth fighting for. They act as quick, accessible reminders of hope and beauty, even during difficult times. The large, medium and small items sit together to occupy the space in our rucksacks. On our backs, they don't weigh us down but, conversely, they lift us up, acting like buoyancy aids.

As each of us is unique, the contents of our rucksacks may vary. Start by mentally designing yours to be unique to you and your life story. Does it have secret pockets for snacks? What colour is it? Is it covered in mud or in pristine condition? I know that mine is a little battered, green, covered in badges from the places I've lived and full of secret zips to hold the loving things my community have said to me over the years.

Sometimes we will need an inventory upgrade. We may slip into an exhaustion and filling our rucksack doesn't provide the level of buoyancy we need. I have been here. In this place, I went for the walks, did the yoga and engaged in the breathwork and I still felt deflated. I sat in puzzling confusion about why my tools weren't working until I realized that in this time and space, I needed different tools: I needed an upgrade. I needed therapeutic support, sharing circles and lengthy social media breaks. The resilience rucksack analogy is just as much about identifying our large, medium and small items as it is about remaining aware that our fluctuating and changing needs might require upgrades.

The exercise at the end of this chapter is the basis for the Resilience Rucksack session in The Resilience Project's Resilience Circles. We begin by journalling around the challenges of engaging with our chosen justice area – what keeps our rucksacks feeling heavy. Some previous examples in climate Circles have been:

- I feel like I need to knowledgeable about everything.
- I feel overwhelmed by information and misinformation.

- I feel like the "climate correspondent" for my friends.
- I feel the guilt of not doing enough.
- I feel like my family don't understand me.
- I don't see other people who look like me in the movement.

We then anonymously write one thing on a sticky note. The group gathers in a circle and take it in turns to read out a different note. If it resonates with you and you agree, you step into the circle, stay for a few seconds, then step back out. It is an exercise to highlight shared experience and anonymously share the dark truths that may sit deep within us. It creates a feeling of being seen, heard and understood and reminds us that we aren't alone in our struggles.

We then repeat the exercise but with the journalling prompt "What helps is . . ." so that we can start to unlock our resilience strategies. Some we've had in the past are:

- Going to the cinema alone
- Asking my friends for help
- Getting a good night's sleep
- Creating zines
- Limiting my time on social media
- Going on a walk, even for ten minutes
- Not looking at my phone first thing in the morning
- Sleeping with my phone in a different room
- Takng a morning walk before I start my day
- Having therapy
- Dancing in my kitchen
- Singing alone in the shower
- Limiting my time spent on the news to 30 minutes a day

The Importance of Discipline

I'm sorry to inform you that discipline is an important part of this story. With its military, self-flagellation and rigid connotations, discipline and resilience may feel like oxymorons, but discipline creates the structure for softness. If you are disciplined in waking up early in the morning, you have more time to carve out space for yourself, before you inhibit the identity of student, worker or changemaker. You might choose to go on a short walk, meditate, exercise or spend time making a delicious breakfast. Discipline is required so that when we feel like crap, we go through our inventory and grab something from our rucksack. We get up and get out of our heads and into our bodies. We call a friend.

Discipline doesn't need to be the stick; it can be the carrot. Through my own ill taste for the military feel of the word discipline, I coined the term "radical encouragement". Discipline may get you out of bed by decreeing that if you don't, you're lazy and a failure. Radical encouragement on the other hand softly says, "Hey, wouldn't it be cool to get up early and watch the sunrise – I know you love sunrises. Heck, how about we go to bed at 9pm so we can get nine hours sleep too?" If you're struggling to find that voice, imagine how your best friend would speak to you. They wouldn't berate and shame you. They would gently nudge you toward actions that you'll be grateful for in the future. Radical encouragement is not the voice of self-hatred, it's the voice of self-compassion and doing things first and foremost not because you should, but because you are in love with yourself. Sometimes, that's chocolate and a film. But sometimes it's training for a half marathon to expand your preconceived limitations; or engaging in the grind of climbing a mountain, to remind yourself that you are a tiny piece of this enormous landscape. We can do discipline without negative self-talk and self-flagellation. Only the discipline that comes with self-love is sustainable. With each of the things in your rucksack, consider, "Am I doing this because I feel inadequate?" or, "Am I doing this because I am in love with myself?"

EXERCISE: THE RESILIENCE RUCKSACK

Objective: This is a reflective group exercise to explore shared challenges (what keeps our rucksacks heavy) and resilience tools (what keeps us light). If you're doing this as an individual, make it a journalling exercise.

Materials needed:

- Journal and pen
- Sticky notes

Step One: Reflection – The Weight We Carry

Journal Prompt:

"What do I find the most difficult things about engaging with my cause?"

Take 5–10 minutes to write freely in your journal. Let the truth come through, even if it feels messy or contradictory.

If in a group, distil one aspect of your reflection onto a single sticky note. Keep it to a sentence or even just a phrase. You won't be attaching your name to it. Place your sticky note anonymously in the centre of the circle formed by the group.

Step Two: Stepping In and Stepping Out (for groups)

Each person in turn draws and reads aloud a sticky note while standing in the circle. After each one is read, if it resonates with you, step into the circle. Stay there for a few breaths in silence, then step back.

Repeat until all notes are read.

Debrief.

Invite optional reflections:

- What did it feel like to hear these truths?
- What did it feel like to see others step in with you?

Step Three: Reflection – What Helps

Now shift the focus to resilience.

Journal Prompt:

"What helps me feel resilient is . . . "

Again, write freely. Then distil one thing that supports your resilience onto a new sticky note.

Step Four: Stepping In and Stepping Out (for groups)

Place the sticky notes in the centre. Repeat the previous process, reading each note aloud and stepping into the circle if it resonates.

As the group witnesses shared strategies, the room will begin to feel a little lighter.

Step Five: Carrying the Rucksack

Now imagine the rucksack you carry with you. It may feel heavy or light on different days. What matters is that we know what helps fill it and that we're not carrying it alone. Visualize putting the rucksack on, with all your intentional practices, and explore what it feels like to embody resilience, strength and balance.

Step Six: Commitment

From all the strategies explored, pick one and commit to trying it out as many days as possible over the next week.

Permission to Have Bad Days

There will be tough days where intentional practice feels too far away. That's okay, there is always tomorrow. Today, remember that we always have the agency to add something to our rucksack, even if it is the smallest item of affirmation, whispering in your ear, "I can do this." Ultimately, building, maintaining and upgrading your Resilience Rucksack is a lifelong practice. It's an evolving commitment to caring for ourselves so we can continue to care for the world around us.

CHAPTER 11:
GUIDEPOST 7 – THE EIGHT TYPES OF REST

"The times are urgent; let us slow down"[40]

Bayo Akomolafe

If Rest was a person, she'd be lying on a sunlounger, cocktail in one hand and book in the other. She'd be blue skies and slow mornings, long walks and knitted jumpers. She'd be *hygge* and perpetually content. "Should" isn't in her vocabulary. She would binge-watch all five series of *Breaking Bad* with no shame. She would enjoy the "fly" episode. She certainly wouldn't be stranded in waves of existential questioning. Step One in learning how to rest is to erase this woman from your memory. Right now.

What stands in the way of meaningful rest is the idea that there is a right and a wrong way to do it. You might have experienced this first hand, when you finally try to rest after an arduous spell at work or school and somehow it feels like your body and mind are working against you. The slumbers aren't deep enough. Your shoulders aren't relaxed enough. Your mind isn't present enough. You're patiently waiting for a calm that doesn't come. Let me introduce your mind beavers: furry little creatures that live in your brain. These clever little fellows live around your mind's streams and rivers – your neural pathways. They build their cognitive dams in different places in your mind, often to hold back certain emotions, thoughts, questions and to keep your mental water levels consistent. Their dam-building materials are often busyness, work, campaigns, hobbies and distractions; all employed to withhold certain things from leaking into the front of your psyche.

Busyness has become an epidemic and our mind beavers have been working overtime. When we were legally required to stop, during the COVID-19 lockdown, our mind beavers still found a way to learn Japanese, run 5km or perfect the sourdough loaf. We were finally afforded some space and rest but for fear of the dams bursting, and having to sit with what is, we were keen to build in new ways of distraction. This is no bad feat. Mind beavers are key architects in upholding a perceived semblance. Rather than intentionally suppressing emotion or thoughts, they are productive little workers attempting to protect you from larger, perhaps more unruly waters. Rest, or seizing their means of production, can therefore be uncomfortable as it disrupts a well-integrated, well-practised and well-respected system of business. Mind beavers have been running a life-time contract in your head and as their bourgeois ruler, you aren't often generous with their holiday allowance. Burnout, the holy grail of beaver union action, calls for change.

Perhaps it's not what Karl Marx would have wanted: to find communism, beavers and our internal cognitive landscape in an analogy. But it illustrates the complex systems in our brains that make slipping into a restful state a little more challenging. The expectation that taking rest is easy is where we often go wrong. This is magnified in the campaigning space, because rest oftens means stopping, which directly contradictions our slogans to "act now". As our work is heart-led, rest can often be accompanied by guilt. Or it can also be understood as "bonus time" to think about strategy, campaigns or how to push for change in your organization. While admittedly great thoughts can come from rest, focusing on the productive outcomes of rest is mind-beaver trickery to dissuade us from prioritizing real, meaningful rest.

Rest Now, Not Later

The phrase "I will rest when …" is more trickery. *I will rest when I've finished this essay or this campaign or this task, or when I have replied to all these emails or WhatsApp messages.* While the intention of rest is a good first step, the "when" mentality delays rest and resilience for the future. The trouble is, once you've replied to those WhatsApp messages, the logic of conversation means that you will get more and your justification that "I will rest when I have replied to the WhatsApp messages" is reignited. If we assume the other person in this exchange subscribes to the same narrative, you will keep replying to messages backward and forward until you or the other person dies!

To exist in the present is to acknowledge that tasks and to-do lists are an unrelenting cycle. Like dusting, wiping your surface once will not safeguard it from debris indefinitely. The dust will come again and the cycle of dusting will, by its very nature, continue forever. So, when rest is parked for the future, the future inevitably stays just that: not the present. Rest is kicked further down the line, sometimes until it's too late.

Rest is Not a Reward

Rather than seeing rest as valuable for our work, we allow it to become a reward for work. Rest is considered a luxury rather than a necessity, often indulged in only after every ounce of effort is wrung out of us. While it is undeniably important to recuperate after intense labour, the benefits of prioritizing rest before and during periods of work are often underestimated.

Like most concepts in this book, I came by the value of rest through my own mistakes and observations. Rest was something I considered to be a "light" topic. It was helpful and "nice" but neither integral nor of spiritual importance. To me, rest was the opposite of productivity; it was synonymous with laziness, immobility, indulgence and lack of discipline. Rest was not compatible with a morning routine, a trip to the gym, a regulated nervous system or a healthy lifestyle. Therefore, in my early twenties I blended rest with "hangover" and "rested me" with "hungover me". My hangover would consist of sleep, trash TV and as many sticks of garlic bread as limbs on my body. Most weekends I was ticking the rest box, yet I wouldn't feel rejuvenated come Monday morning.

When my body pushed me into a state of *enforced* rest rather than *optional* rest around my first burnout, my examination was revived out of necessity. As I had redefined rest as the opposite of being productive, I first adopted the hangover mentality: sofa, horizontal body position, chick-flicks, propping my head up on a battalion of garlic breads. For me, this didn't feel as relaxing as I had anticipated. Why? Because lying on the sofa all day gave my mind space to run rampant, and what I truly needed was rest from my *mind*. I needed to stop thinking about planetary demise and campaigns and global politics. My enquiry led me to find an understanding of rest beyond taking a bath or the evening off or even going to the spa. I don't attempt to devalue these as modalities of self-care; for me they are helpful and kind and wonderful, but not *deeply* restful. I knew that I was struggling with over-thinking, rumination and not knowing who I was beyond campaigning. As my rest was coming from exhaustion, I started thinking not around what was "restful" but "What activities increase my vitality?" Lying on the sofa did not. But climbing mountains did.

All these thinkings, from mountains to TV to cognitive beaver-communism, has led me to the work of Dr Saundra Dalton-Smith, a US academic who introduced the idea that there are, in fact, seven types of rest. I chowed down on this concept, but hungry for an extra course and its relevance to activism, I worked with an international group of youth activists to introduce an eighth type of rest, which we imperfectly named "identity rest".

The Eight Types of Rest

Dr Saundra Dalton-Smith broke ground by demonstrating that rest encompasses much more than simply shutting our eyes. She broke down rest into seven categories: physical, mental, sensory, creative, emotional, social and spiritual.

1. Physical Rest

Physical rest is perhaps the most familiar form and is comprised of both passive and active components. Passive physical rest includes the essential act of sleeping and napping, of which you might need eight to then hours daily. A more active physical rest involves activities that promote relaxation and recovery, such as gentle stretching, yoga or massage. Many people mistakenly equate rest solely with sleep. Dr Dalton-Smith emphasizes that sufficient quality sleep is just one part of physical restoration. Other examples of physical rest could include tai chi, gentle walks in nature or other activities that regulate your nervous system.

2. Mental Rest

Mental rest addresses the exhaustion caused by overthinking, constant decision-making and cognitive overload. This can be especially prevalent for campaigners and anyone working in social justice. It is not uncommon to hear of youths lying awake at night with racing thoughts about the world and struggling to focus during the day. To combat mental fatigue, she suggests incorporating mental breaks throughout the day, moments where the brain is free from intense concentration. Other activities include mindfulness, meditation, journalling, using a pocket diary to clear mental clutter or simply pausing work for a short, undistracted break outside.

3. Sensory Rest

Our sensory attention is constantly occupied, from the glow of screens and flashing notifications to the incessant hum of urban life. Sensory overload leads to fatigue, irritability and even physical symptoms like headaches. Sensory rest involves intentionally reducing stimuli to give our senses a chance to recover. This can include dimming lights, muting unnecessary noise, setting aside technology-free time or stepping into nature. Sensory rest is what we achieve through our digital detoxes.

4. Creative Rest

Creative rest is essential for those who engage in problem-solving, brainstorming or laptop work. The pressure to continuously innovate can leave people feeling uninspired and mentally blocked. Dr Dalton-Smith proposes that creative rest involves exposing yourself to sources of inspiration and awe, such as art and nature or engaging with beauty. Spending time outdoors, appreciating music or visiting a gallery can help reignite the spark of creativity and foster a sense of wonder. For those feeling creatively spent, creative rest restores their ability to generate new ideas and think imaginatively.

5. Emotional Rest

Emotional rest means having the freedom to express your true feelings without fear of judgement, guilt or repercussion. Many people feel emotionally drained by the expectations of social roles or by suppressing their emotions to avoid conflict. Dr Dalton-Smith advises seeking authentic connections with trusted individuals and giving yourself permission to share honestly and without masks. It also includes creating boundaries that reduce emotional labour, such as limiting interactions with draining people. In building a youth group to be one of care and compassion, you are fostering a sense of emotional rest, even if meeting together puts a strain on your calendar.

6. Social Rest

Social rest is closely related to emotional rest but focuses on the dynamics of social interactions. It involves recognizing those relationships that energize us and those that drain us. Resting socially doesn't necessarily mean isolation; rather, it means choosing to engage with people who provide positive energy and support, while setting boundaries with relationships that demand more than they give. Intentional solitude or seeking out supportive connections can fulfil social rest needs, especially for those who often find themselves feeling stretched thin in their social roles.

7. Spiritual Rest

Spiritual rest is about feeling a deep sense of belonging, purpose and connection beyond oneself. For some, this comes through religious faith, meditation, community service or practising mindfulness. Engaging in activities that align with one's values, volunteering or fostering a connection to something greater can provide profound spiritual fulfilment and peace. Spiritual rest can be understood as anything that allows people to reflect on their purpose and meaning.

8. Identity Rest

The model of the seven types of rest, while incredibly powerful, didn't seem to wholly connect with the unique experience of young people striving for climate and social justice. So, I worked to co-design an eighth type with changemakers from 18 different countries to address these deficiencies. They coined something called "identity rest". For changemakers, this involves stepping away from the roles and expectations society places upon them to be the generation to fix our problems. Identity rest is acknowledging that living in the polycrisis and being constantly visible leads us to occupy certain roles and identities, which come with set expectations. Living up to supposed expectations can weigh heavily on our energy reserves. If, say, you're trying to be the "perfect climate activist", this will leave you falling short of your own and others' expectations 90 per cent of the time, due to the structures of modern living. For example, you will almost inevitably buy plastic, be that the container your tomatoes come in, a drink in your meal deal or your contact lenses. You might need to take a flight and you might also buy something that unbeknown to you involved exploitative conditions because capitalism is great at hiding injustice.

Identity rest is putting down the "activist" or "youth changemaker" or "facilitator" or "wise counsel" title momentarily and being a more expansive expression of ourselves, with space to be flawed and imperfect. In practical terms, this could look like resting from the expectations of "virtue". You might rest from the expectation that you should be posting about every conflict in the world. It could be enjoying meat culturally or at Christmas or flying on a special holiday with your family. Identity rest is not giving up, it's not ruining the planet and it's not betraying the movement – it's uncovering a deeper form of rest *as a means to* further sustain your movement, advocacy or change.

Of course, the term "identity rest" is fraught with difficulty. If your identity is marginalized, oppressed or scapegoated, resting from who you are is not a choice nor an option. Your identity may also be a source of pride. We recognized this tension and leave the title of this rest as the user's choice. What "identity" aptly captures is allowing individuals to strip back the projections of who they are "supposed to be" – to recharge without constantly performing the role of "the advocate", "the fighter" or "the leader". Taking time to just be who you are, beyond the crises around us, is a powerful, transformative form of respite. When is the last time you did something entirely for *you*?

Denial Days

After my own burnout, I was lying on a UK beach with my friends when I started to develop the concept of denial days, which are similar to holiday days or annual leave. Just like time off, they are a set number of days where you're given permission to switch off from the world and prioritize yourself. This means no listening to the news, no chat about your justice area and no checking notifications.

A part of my 21-year-old self wrestles back to this sentiment. She shrieks, "The privilege of it all! How dare you suggest we deny structures literally killing people. For so many there is no option for denial days! 'Denial' has cost our movement years." And there is another part of 21-year-old me, the most tender part, whispering back, "Thank you for giving me permission to rest. I want to go to the beach with my friends today and talk about Little Mix." To be clear, denial days are not permission for apathy. They are specific and time bound. They are chosen dates in the calendar where you get to install your software updates (more on that next). They are *in service* of your life, your vitality and your activism, not in contradiction of them. Sometimes we need to switch off to fully switch back on.

Take a moment to think about what a denial day would look like for you. What feels like it nourishes the you beyond activism? It might involve time with friends from home or muting/archiving group chats. Could you factor a denial day into a birthday gift you'd like to ask for, like seeing a musical, going to a gig or a day trip away? In this way, self-care starts to look far more expansive than a bath or a run. It becomes a cognitive and intentional decision we are proactively making, rather than passively consuming.

TATT – Tired All the Time

"Rest" has evolved into an amorphous, catch-all term. The same is true for the most used word in the English vernacular: tired, which has become so overused and unspecific that it's hard not to go a day without hearing it. Everyone is tired. My friend, a doctor, said there is even an acronym for it they use: TATT (tired all the time). This friend claims he sees six to eight patients per day who have TATT. We've become so accustomed to using this word that we've neglected to further interrogate it. From a medical perspective, tiredness is a symptom of a never-ending list of various psychological, physiological and somatic happenings. Instead of simply treating the symptom, discerning the root cause is likely to have a longer lasting impact.

To begin this process, instead of your starting point being, "I'm tired, what can I do about it?", I invite you to begin with a different question: not "What do I need?" but "Where are my deficiencies?"If you eat a largely plant-based diet, you might be deficient in iron or vitamin B12. So, get a blood test. Also sleep – it has magical powers. Covering your basics – food, sleep, water, nutrition – is an overlooked starting point, but it's where I always begin. When you run into fatigue, resist the urge to fix it and first consider your sleep quality, the food you've eaten and how much water you've drunk.

EXERCISE: WHY AM I TIRED ALL THE TIME?

Objective: Once you've got your basics sorted, try to pinpoint the root cause of your tiredness.

Step One: What Is on My Plate Right Now?

Firstly, understand, name and write down everything that is on your plate, from personal to professional. Include the big questions and the small tasks. Nothing is too small – if it's bothering you, write it down! Starting here allows us to see all our stresses on the page and perhaps bring ourselves a shade of compassion when we witness how much we're holding. In detailing what's on your plate, you can begin to explore how you feel about all these obstacles, relationships and challenges.

Step Two: Where Are My Deficiencies?

Consider overshoot (excess) and undershoot (deficiencies). We are often in overshoot with work, social commitments, our diet and stress, and undershoot in core requirements for the human spirit, such as play, creativity, connection, nature and fun. Consider the following examples of where your deficiencies may be.

- Long hours and multiple deadlines in sedentary work will leave you tired as you're not being active, so when was the last time you engaged in play or creative rest?
- Dreaming up your own impact project will leave you tired, as it is heavy to hold all that on your own, so are you deficient in friendship and support or emotional rest?
- Running a home and a family will leave you tired because there are multiple demands on your time, so are you deficient in nourishing yourself the you beyond those demands? Is there a deficiency in your relationship with

yourself, or "me time" or identity rest? When is the last time you did something just for you?

- Social media will leave you tired because it's information overload. When did you last disengage from the digital sphere and immerse yourself in nature or sensory rest?

Step Three: What Do the Many "Me–s" Need?

Time may be linear, but your body is a hotel housing all of the past "yous". They all live inside you and they all have needs. Inside me there is a 26-year-old who, in giving so much of herself to others, feels that she needs to hide away in solitude to reclaim her own soul. There is a 23-year-old who is devoted to acting on climate. There is a 20-year-old who loves a party and seeing the sun rise. And there is a very soft, sensitive little girl, unaware that her sensitivity will be devalued by the world she's born into.

Sometimes I feel "tired" because these precious and flawed women are not being heard or nourished. For example, when I'm deep in work-mode, living a virtuous sober, vegan life, my party girl cries out that she is craving wildness or adventure. There are many "yous" inside you too. Ask yourself:

- Who are the different versions of me existing inside me?
- Who is my small child? What does she long for?
- Who is my teenager? What do they long for?
- What am I deficient in (see Step 2)? How can I start to incorporate these things into my life?

Installing Our Spiritual Software Updates

For all our arrogance, humans need updating too. After four intense years of dedicated work, growing The Resilience Project from a tiny seed to an international organization, navigating funding crises every cycle and personal stress outside my 9–5, I took a big chunk of rest in pursuit of the GROWTH Recovery Arc from Guidepost 5. With the support of my team, I took five weeks off and spent it chewing through these different forms of rest and really experiencing each of their impact on my body. I spent three days walking alone on the west coast of Scotland to explore physical and mental rest, crying alone in the hills when I realized that there was nothing "gentle" about this rest and I needed more softness. I also made time to visit my friends, gossiping over wine, stoking my identity rest of the virtuous activist. I made a lot of cakes, creatively resting. Some days I woke up at 6:30am and meditated. Some days I lay in until 11am and blissfully stayed in my pyjamas all day. These activities neither cost hundreds of pounds nor were hidden in exotic holidays. I didn't do a ten-day vipassana or a pilgrimage or a therapeutic course or laughter yoga. I let joy and enjoyment guide me. I did not strive. Did not make goals. Did not excel. Did not pursue. I slowed down and reflected, yes, but more importantly I enjoyed enjoying my life. That was my mantra. Enjoy *enjoying* your life.

Over the weeks, I noticed changes taking place – better sleep, reduced cravings for sugar and a lighter spirit. Friends saw it too; they commented on the spark in my eyes and the calmness in my demeanour. Of course, not everyone can take five weeks off – in fact that's very rare. What I advocate now in my life, working full time, is finding the small spaces where I can enjoy enjoying my life. This involves keeping at least two evenings free each week to prioritize the rest I need that day.

Any time of extended rest, non-striving or denial days, I liken to the body installing its psychological, spiritual and emotional software updates. Life moves at such an unrelenting pace that it's easy to move from experience to experience without allowing the learnings to metabolize in the body. We change but we don't notice. Sometimes change is obvious: dramatic life moments shift us instantly, pulling the ground from beneath our feet. Smaller moments can accumulate quietly, changing us without us even noticing. They can catch us off guard where we think, *Where has the time gone? When did I change?* Often this is a positive change; we become more self-assured as we age without even noticing or we become confident and proud in our difference. But other times, it can be less positive; the "work" takes over our personal life; we become alienated from those who don't agree with our views; we become a version of who we think we should be rather than who we are deep down.

Installing your software updates is reclaiming time to simply be and process. When we look at our domestic landscape, maintenance is everywhere. We oil our bike chains, service our cars and pour salt in the dishwasher. We even replace our lightbulbs once in a while. They are required for smoother domestic life. Our internal life is no different and also requires maintenance. In the case of my phone, its software updates happen a few times a year. I am required to plug it into a power source and allow it the time it needs to pause and work its behind-the-scenes magic. Come morning, it's installed.

While we certainly aren't machines, perhaps in this instance we can pinch some wisdom from our gadgets. In the case of my own rest, I followed the phone instruction manual protocol. I knew software updates were needed. It was time to switch off and plug into the mains. I found that my power source was laughing with my friends, being with my family and spending time alone in nature, challenging my earlier conceptions of where I thought I got my energy from. I thought energy came from the climate movement, praise at work, campaign wins and positive climate news. While these are without doubt extraordinarily energizing, in my life they had only provided fleeting and temporary surges. Rather, laughing wildly with my best friend and being held by the person I love has provided a richer form of energy. What is love, if not plugging into the cosmic mains?

I found that qualifying my "no's" (to non-essential requests on my time and spirit), with, "Sorry, am installing my software updates", was a powerful and amusing practice. In a campaign setting, this could be setting fierce boundaries on rest time and carving out quality, uniquely enriching "you" time. Then, find your sustainable power source. It may differ from person to person, but I have a hunch that across the board it's about people; about being loved, seen, heard and understood by those you trust. Find your version of the mains, plug in and let your body do the rest. This can be over a weekend, in a morning or integrating more "mains" time into your week. You might be surprised what you find. Perhaps the solution to the degradation of the soul is the reclamation of the soul.

Find the kind of rest that will lead you to vitality. Not "How do I feel less tired?" but "How do I feel more alive?" For me, it's the secrets I whisper to the ridges of the mountains, hundreds of miles from a hearing ear. It's sharing tears over the kitchen table with my best friends and letting them in to my most vulnerable and soft side. It's giving something life, either tending house plants, growing vegetables or nurturing a project from seed to idea, regardless of "success" or "impact". It's not Gmail, or hyper efficiency or even filling Moleskine diaries. It's taking that first moment of the day to appreciate the sun on my skin, holding my husband's hand under the pillow as we sleep, breathing in all the possibility of today and the gratitude for yesterday.

Find the kind of rest that will lead you to vitality.

CHAPTER 12:

GUIDEPOST 8 – GRATITUDE WITHOUT NUMBING

"We are all more blind to what we have than to what we have not."[41]

Audre Lorde

Gratitude often has a bad reputation. It can be misunderstood as toxic positivity, "good vibes only" and a New Age justification to not look at the hard stuff. Yet we're reminded as a generation to be consistently grateful. We should be grateful to live in a time where we are far less likely to die from tuberculosis, aren't sent to war and aren't peasants in feudal times. Rightly so. In 2024, I attended a talk from acclaimed dystopia fiction writer Margaret Atwood. Candidly she said, "Cheer up, it's been worse – once there were no avocados in North America." Received with laughter and a huge round of applause, she continued, "The bubonic plague killed half the population of europe, there were European diseases that killed 80 per cent of the North and South American populations, the 1918–20 flu pandemic killed 50 million people. Cheer up, it's been worse".[42] Atwood is right and it's a sobering reminder that we should be fundamentally grateful for our access to safety and security. But at the same time, that should not pacify us into accepting how things are.

In movements grounded in fierce urgency, the invitation to pause and feel grateful might be dangerous. My response to gratitude, both in its capacity for tone deaf optimism and its ability to minimize struggle, was a growing distrust. Gratitude felt like an anaesthetic for things we should not tolerate. Too much gratitude will surely deaden our desire to mobilize and campaign against systemic inequalities. Too little gratitude and we close ourselves off to contentedness, perspective and appreciation. But when my physical health became compromised by burnout, I knew that nuance existed beyond the binary, and that gratitude and I needed to have a deeper conversation.

Gratitude as Spiritual Bypass

I first became aware of the term "spiritual bypass" in therapy for my eating disorder. Yep, it wasn't a phrase gently explained to me, it was a diagnosis. Spiritual bypassing was coined by psychologist John Welwood in the 1980s to describe the tendency to use spiritual ideas and practices to sidestep or avoid facing unresolved emotional issues, psychological wounds or uncomfortable social realities. Welwood observed this especially in Western spiritual communities, where people would gravitate toward transcendent ideals like love, light, oneness or gratitude as a way of avoiding the messiness of their own pain or the complexity of relationships. In short: narrowing in on the good stuff can protect us from the hard, uncomfortable stuff.

I witnessed this firsthand in spiritual communities during my time living in Australia, aged 20. I had become more interested in meditation as a route to self-knowledge and as I was there alone, I was also deeply in need of some mates. I found myself swimming in new circles of seemingly liberated people, absorbing some of the learnings from their counter-current lifestyles. I did learn a lot, but the honeymoon phase – the singing, the dancing and the joy – faded into frustration. I was rendered speechless when one self-proclaimed wise spirit recommended meditation as a solution to the genocide of Aboriginal peoples. He suggested that if we all meditated then hate would not prevail and when I pressed a bit harder, he questioned why we were spending our energy on "bad vibes". I understood his sentiment and the deep yearning for a solution to be so simple, but meditation as the only solution is working to a timescale we don't have, nor does it address reparations and justice.

That experience wasn't the only one. The phrases "Everything happens for a reason" and "Trust the universe", and the term "manifestation" seemed commonplace, but they overlooked the asymmetric cards people are dealt all over the world. The final straw was hearing that climate change was the Earth healing itself, without mention of the innocent lives given to generate such healing. It was easier to wish away the climate crisis as a cosmic force than to confront the reality of it being caused by humans and a death sentence for millions. While meditation, dance and yoga felt nourishing for me personally, I grew disillusioned with some of the people I was meeting who were so loud about "one love" but so quiet on social justice.

Now I was sitting in a poky therapy room in Bristol, age 23, with Jeanette listening to my burnout story, cocking her head and cautiously asking, "Have you heard of spiritual bypass?"

"Yes!" I cooed enthusiastically. "Let me tell you about Australia! When I was . . ."

She interrupted. "No. I think we should talk about you." Huh?

Spiritual bypassing, while seemingly the realm of New Age spiritualists and men with manbuns, also becomes relevant in spaces of activism and social change. Many changemakers come into movement spaces with a strong sense of responsibility. We're driven by care, anger and vision. We show up for protests, petitions, mutual aid efforts and organizing communities, though if we're not on the front lines or getting arrested, we often dismiss our own exhaustion or pain. We tell ourselves we have no right to be tired or upset, that others have it worse, that if we just focused on what we should be grateful for, we wouldn't feel so depleted. This might show up in narratives like, "Others have it worse so I shouldn't complain", "I have no right to feel burned out, I'm not doing nearly as much as others" or, "I live in the UK, I can't be burned out."

In the same way that "love" was being used to check-out of the external strife in spiritual communities in Australia, "gratitude" and "wellness" can be used to check out of our internal strife in changemaking spaces. Spiritual tools become a way to override the body's signals. Tools like mindfulness and meditation are used to nullify and eradicate stress rather than uncover the truths that lie beneath them. Rest gets framed as indulgence. Burnout is seen as a personal failure – you're not meditating enough, engaging in wellness enough or staying grateful enough – rather than as a systemic condition.

In that room in Bristol, I couldn't even use the word "burnout". I felt like burnout didn't happen to someone like me. Not only did I consider myself as resilient and having a strong wellness practice, but I actually held the title of Wellbeing Officer for my campaign groups. So, when explaining my story, I peppered every bit of my descent into bulimia with addendums that nodded to my gratitude. "I have a lot to be grateful for. I have great friends. I'm not in the countries where rising sea levels are destroying my home. I have financial security. So really, nothing is *that* bad, I'm just here because of a few minor issues." While these statements are objectively true and merit gratitude, my overidentification with them was a way of bypassing the truth – that I had to admit I was burned out and my hunger to be the perfect citizen, sister, partner and changemaker was benefitting others more than myself.

When we bypass our own limits in the name of strength or resilience, we slowly disconnect from our bodies, our boundaries and ultimately from our capacity to stay doing the work. The truth is, you don't need to be on the front lines to need rest. You don't need to be publicly leading to deserve care.

Gratitude Isn't an Exit, It's a Doorway to Meaning

Routinely identifying the relationships, people and basic human rights that enable our quality of life reminds us of what we are fighting for and what we have to lose. For changemakers, it reconnects us to the "why" of what we do. Rather than soften our edge, gratitude can sharpen our focus. Gratitude is not a thick curtain that hides the challenges we face but a clear pane of glass through which we can see challenge differently.

We sharpen our focus by embracing both/and. Recall Guidepost 3, where emotions can co-exist. We can hold both gratitude *and* grief, where gratitude doesn't dilute grief but helps us hold it. Gratitude softens the intensity of grief, and the reality of loss encourages us to appreciate the small things. Rather than opposing forces, they are mutually reinforcing. Sometimes I want to turn away from grief, hide my head in the sand and look purely at the love I find in my little life. I want to bury my head in a book and not think at all about the world. Other times I want to devote my entire life and energy to service, because what's the point if not to progress? I have found that neither strategy helps on its own. The work is not to look away from all that we stand to lose but to expand our gaze to encompass all that we have, all that we gain. That's why we have two eyes.

We can hold both gratitude *and* grief.

EXERCISE: TEN-FINGER GRATITUDE

Objective: The Ten-Finger Gratitude exercise is a simple, grounding practice where you pause and, using each of your ten fingers, name one thing for each finger that you're grateful for, big or small.

It could be the warmth of sunlight, a person, clean water or a delicious meal. The goal isn't perfection or depth, but presence: to gently shift your attention from stress or scarcity to appreciation, building a daily habit of noticing what's still good, even in hard times.

Hunt for the Good Stuff

Critical scrutiny is an essential skill, often rewarded at university and praised in the social change sector. Powerful social movements have been built through casting a critical gaze over existing systems, structures and resource allocation. Even neurologically, our brains have evolved with a negativity bias, a survival function that prioritizes threat, criticism and failure so we can protect ourselves. All three of these examples have life-changing potential. But have they become so hardwired that we have lost the art of acknowledging the good? If so, we retrain our attention.

It may seem that there are more things in the 21st century that are wrong rather than right. The idea of Hunting for the Good Stuff, introduced to me by Dr Chris Johnstone, is to resist our negativity bias and to see the light too. Research by psychologist Dr Robert Emmons, one of the world's leading scholars on gratitude, has shown that people who journal their gratitude regularly experience stronger immune systems, better sleep and deeper feelings of connection to others.

The final step of the eight-week programme is all about reflection and gratitude. At The Resilience Project young people gather in Resilience Circles and retrain their attention, contemplating what they are grateful to this community for, writing each other anonymous love letters. It's a beautiful practice and some of the most precious memories of my life are of sitting on a hill at our Resilience Residential, listening to young campaigners sharing their gratitude with each other. As Grace said of her 2021 experience, "My life is happier, healthier, more connected, informed and filled with joy, love, hope and strength because of this amazing project and, if everyone got to experience this, the world would be too." You can feel the impact of gratitude in the exercise below, a variation of the exercise in our eight-week model, but powerful nonetheless.

EXERCISE: WRITE A GRATITUDE LETTER

Objective: The Gratitude Letter experiment, designed by Dr Martin Seligman, tests how intentional acts of gratitude affect wellbeing and happiness. The "gratitude visit" involves writing a letter to someone you've never properly thanked.

Materials needed:

- A timer (phone, watch or clock)
- A laptop or smartphone (preferable) or a notebook and pen

Step One: Write The Letter (8-10 minutes)

Think of someone you never properly thanked: an old teacher, a mentor, a friend, a family member, or perhaps someone who has really helped or inspired you during your changemaking journey.

Spend 8 minutes writing a letter that includes:

- What they did for you
- Why it meant so much
- How it affected your life

Step Two: Send the letter (1 minute)

After writing, send the letter. This might be sending it as an e-mail or a text or planning when you'll go to the post office to send it.

Step Three: Group debrief or solo reflection (5–10 minutes)

If you're in a group, gather everyone today. If you're doing this alone, spend some time reflecting in your journal on the following:

- What did you notice? What feelings came up? Did anything surprise you?
- What does this say about how we sustain ourselves and each other?
- How might practising gratitude in this way support your changemaking?

PART THREE

CHAPTER 13:

WHY WE REPEAT – MY SECOND BURNOUT

If the Act is our spirit, the Rest is our soul, the Reset is our mind, then the Repeat is our humanity. We repeat because life will be an endless journey of meeting and re-meeting who we are in response to changing external conditions. Inside and outside of changemaking, we will meet stress, sadness, despair, hope, love and wonder. Growth is not linear; instead, we move through perpetual cycles of becoming and unbecoming. You may identify from your own life a time of great difficulty, when you made changes to better serve your life and minimize your own suffering. Then later in life, when meeting difficulty again, you may have slipped back into deep psychological patterns that furthered suffering. Common patterns changemakers struggle to escape include self-sacrifice (martyrdom), people-pleasing and tying achievement to worth.

Growth is not linear; instead, we move through perpetual cycles of becoming and unbecoming.

A second reason for suffering is that sometimes we change, but everything else stays the same. Jade was one of the first young climate activists to move through our eight-week programme and attend the Resilience Residential.

For her, it was life-changing. It catalysed a break-up, a change of job and a deepened understanding of who she is and how she shows up in this world. What she wasn't anticipating was that while she'd changed, the world and her communities had not. Jade emerged from the programme feeling empowered and revitalized, but landed back into the same family unit (who didn't believe in climate change), the same toxic activist group (who glorified burnout) and the same routine (which lacked access to nature). We can change our inner landscapes while our outer container might remain the same. Naturally, when loneliness and sadness overwhelmed her, it felt like a personal regression, like she was back to square one. It took Jade time to realize that the "real" work was not simply uncovering emotional, social and psychological learnings during the programme, but how she could stay true to them throughout the stress and complexity of modern life. She had to learn not just to talk about different ways of campaigning, but to model it. She had to protect her fire and find out how to integrate her new learnings into her same life, within her financial, social and cultural container.

Why Do We Repeat?

What's important to recognize is that when we absorb a changemaking blow or feel a great sense of regression after proactively engaging in work to support ourselves, we aren't back to square one. Rather than growth being a straight line, it's a spiral. We move round the spiral from a central point, and any set back doesn't move us back to the beginning, rather we jump back to a lower rung. This rung is still outwards from where we began, but not back to the beginning. Integration and how we transition back into the world becomes paramount to ensure that resilience isn't confined to the eight-week programme, and that it becomes the connective tissue that underpins our lives. These guideposts become less of a toolkit for action and more of a framework for living.

Consider the way we tend to our exterior life, such as our homes and our bodies. We stay in shape through routine and sustained physical exertion. We cut our hair regularly, clean our kitchens almost daily and make our bed each morning. These repeated rituals support maintenance, balance and presentation. Yet when it comes to our interior life, we offer far less attention. We then act surprised when we find ourselves getting into the same situations. Activities that support mental fitness, such as retreats, peer support programmes, meditation and philosophical frameworks, are still fringe activities. They also sit behind enormous paywalls. We have few readily available structures for internal maintenance and therapy is expensive. It's no wonder that our sense of resilience erodes. It's no wonder Jade felt deflated after the programme. Repeat therefore, becomes essential, not as a step we tick off but as an integration into the rest of our lives. How will you weave mental fitness maintenance into your own life? Will you start your own Resilience Circle? Or devote yourself to journalling, peer support or another routine exercise that reveals your essence? We repeat because sustained effort reaps rewards.

We also repeat because life is unpredictable. What keeps you strong and stable now will change in response to changing conditions. You may be thrown a curveball that compromises your changemaking. You might experience a crushing setback, inside or out of the Arena. I learned that during my second burnout.

My Second Burnout

At age 26 I had designed the Resilience Residential, bringing together 14 youth activists from across the UK to a week-long immersive retreat. In between the wild swimming, campfire singing and nature time, I was training them to deliver our Climate Activation model in their local areas. They'd be building and facilitating their own Resilience Circles, though I'd guest facilitate the burnout session as I was considered the resident expert after my own burnout and my long investigation into it. The idea was that I would lead the session for all seven Circles, working my way around the UK to visit each. But it didn't work out that way.

The Residential a group of 20 somethings met in the year after the global pandemic. We were hashing out the expectation placed upon us in 2019, the experience of being arrested and detained and the feelings of isolation from friends and family who didn't "get" it. As you can imagine, it was incredibly emotional, with all the participants exposing their scars to the light and finding the beginnings of deep healing. We cried together every single day – in sadness, in grief and in gratitude.

I will never forget sitting in the kitchen with one of them one late afternoon. We talked for so long that the sun set, and we sat speaking softly in the darkness, barely able to make out each other's faces. In the anonymity of darkness, which felt more like the womb than the grave, they confided in me how they had been suicidal the year prior and that they'd never, until this moment, told anyone. Being trusted with something like that is a memory I'll keep with me forever, and it pressed into me the knowing that spaces where we can feel seen and understood have a nurturing power beyond any workshop, mnemonic or podcast. That moment all those years ago was life-changing for both of us.

During the Residential we sat in nature, and I listened to the fears and frustrations that I too felt as a 26-year-old. Holding this space, teaching the course and keeping everything on time was an enormous undertaking, but one I felt ready for. Eustress enabled me to feel focused, energized and extraordinary, every single day. Recognizing that I'd run an emotional ultramarathon, a crash began to feel inevitable.

Fortunately, I'd been through my own Act, Rest, Reset, Repeat and I knew that I needed rest, acceptance and a huge helping of joy and laughter. I intentionally decided to travel back from the Residential via the funniest man I've ever known, voted "funniest boy" two years running in his sixth form – my wonderful brother, Chris. He is not an activist. Chris is a larger-than-life character who, unlike me, wears contentedness like a well-fitting jacket. He has always been the light in the room, has always injected joy into any group setting. His life is playful, and his company and lightness have kept me grounded for many years. Going to his house and watching wrestling together has always been a welcome escape from the busyness of my mind, nourishing the angry bit of me that just wants to sit and watch one man bash in the head of another with a metal chair. Being with Chris was exactly what I needed in response to a week of peering at existential doom.

When I arrived, I dropped my bags on the floor, gave big hugs and waited for a cup of tea. Chris stood in the kitchen and said to me "So … how was it?" I clearly remember the way his eyes crinkled as he smiled, nervously tapping his fingers on the table. I fumbled my way through the sensemaking process I hadn't yet begun. How could I summarize such a magnanimous, transformational experience? It turns out that I didn't need to, because a few sentences in, Chris interrupted me and in true older brother style said, "Yes, but I have something I want to tell you." I threw my head back with a knowing and welcome laugh. On the car journey down I'd been playing out the scene on my arrival: he'd ask me one question about the Residential, say, "Well done, I'm proud of you", then launch into updates on his own life, in the way only a sibling could.

"I knew you'd do this! Go on, tell me!" I cackled.

He looked down at his hands and then into my eyes. "I've been diagnosed with lymphoma."

Time waivered for a moment as my mind tried to recall if lymphoma was cancer or some kind of Latin word for the flu.

I said, "Okay" and sat there, quite stunned. A pause hung in the air as he said "You … took that very well."

Denial took the reins and I batted back nonchalantly, "Yeah, honestly I don't know what lymphoma is."

The word cancer was gently thrown back to me, and without knowing what to do, we both started laughing in the way that only siblings can. There is no rule book for when your only sibling tells you he has cancer off the back of a week where you feel like you've been living in a utopian community, where the possibility of life seemed unlimited. There is no guidance on the tremendous amount of emotional whiplash you will experience when you're dragged back into the finite limits of life itself. I asked him if he could find me a cigarette to smoke even though I was not a smoker, and we sat outside playing house music thinking through if he could reasonably ask the Make a Wish foundation for an Xbox 360 at the age of 29. No tears spilled. I asked questions. He answered. I asked him questions only a sibling could: whether he was a little bit excited to confront his own death. On the drive home to Bristol, I started screaming in my car halfway down the M4. I could not stop. I could not stop screaming.

The next three months were a whirlwind. The first month consisted of a further investigation, which found that unfortunately an error had been made and fortunately Chris did not have cancer. Relief flooded through our bodies, even as my mum was firmer in her conviction that it had never been cancer to begin with, something I had assumed was denial. But the stress on our bodies had already been sewed into our skin. No misdiagnoses could undo the fear and tension our nervous systems had been storing all these weeks. Life and work continued, but my body was still playing catch-up. In the second month, Chris, still struggling, was admitted back into hospital and the c-word began creeping back into conversations. That week, after a semi-diagnosis we were told again that it was unlikely it was cancer. He stayed in hospital for further testing.

Finally, when Life had exhausted its will-they-won't-they performance of summer 2021, Chris was formally diagnosed with a rare form of neck cancer, in the third month after his crinkled eyes had shone in his kitchen. While I sat in stone at home, Chris, Mum and Dad were sitting with an oncologist who said that if his treatment plan didn't work, there was nothing the doctors could do for him.

As a founder, I didn't take off this time of backward and forward diagnoses. I didn't feel I could. In fact, I threw myself into work. I knew that if I stopped, the work stopped, and I needed to assist those 14 individuals and the 7 support communities they were building across the UK. Though I'd worked to break patterns of prioritizing others over myself, this experience resurrected old coping mechanisms. As my own world crumbled, I needed to engender these warm, soft and loving communities to meet an unmet need in myself.

The burden to keep going fell solely on my shoulders, as I moved closer to 2022, with no funding on the horizon and no team around me. At the same time, I was still doing my volunteer activism preparing for COP26. I was meeting my team weekly, knowing full well that Chris would start chemo on the first day of the conference in Glasgow – the very same day where this book begins, finding myself in a meeting room with a senior negotiator, out of patience and ready to take more risks. During this time, life evaded me. Life moved around me and about me, but not within me, a feeling I imagine is exclusive to ghosts and those of us who periodically slip through the cracks. Time slowed down and time sped up. When I partied, I partied hard. I slept late. I didn't shower. But I also put into practice all the things I knew helped. I signed up for therapy, engaged in more yoga and started saying no to most things. I was doing all the "things" I delivered workshops on, but they didn't provide the anaesthetic I was craving, adding on layers of guilt and imposter syndrome to an already complex picture.

Around the second misdiagnosis, and on the back of a very heavy hangover, my body moved into a state of breakdown. The crying seemed endless. My emotions seemed three steps ahead of me: I'd be laughing one day, motivated to sign up for meditation and exercise classes the next, yet on others my body lacked the energy to get out of bed. My mind and body started moving with disharmony and I felt like I'd cracked. I took two weeks off work and stared longingly at the Welsh sea, envious of the waves that were forever granted the grace to break and begin again.

When Chris's third and final diagnosis came through, I started to feel not just better, but counterintuitively the best I'd felt in ages. We had a roadmap and I had a motivation: resource myself to be the best support I can be. I started a meditation course with a meditation tutor, began therapy and asked my friends for support. As Chris moved through chemotherapy and radiotherapy we bought him small presents for each week of treatment he completed and gathered as a strong family unit. When I was alone, I allowed myself to say yes to sadness and grief, stepping back from activism and making a pact with myself to be okay with falling short of others' expectations.

I breathe in gratitude from the bottom of my toes that Chris responded positively to treatment. Almost one year later, he was cancer free. Now three years later, he delights in a life of marriage and children. I know this is not the same outcome for all. In the long journey of holding my breath, I needed to fill my lungs. I left the city and made a bold move to the Scottish Highlands, where I didn't know a single person. Because sometimes when we look inside, we find that the tools we have fall short. This is why we repeat again and again and again like rolling tides. Sometimes you must find more strategies to meet your deficiencies. Unlike previous years, where I'd needed connection, in 2022 I knew deep down I needed space and anonymity, so I was able to move to the middle of nowhere where nobody knew me, to cry in the mountains. In that space I found that *I* was the wave, and I had the strength to break and begin again.

The Grace to Begin Again

This experience taught me many things. Changemakers do not exist in a vacuum. Your viewpoint may feel global, but your day to day will be impacted by your relationships, your mindset and your life circumstance. With this in mind, we must give ourselves grace. We don't step into the Arena and leave the rest of ourselves at the door. We bring our scars, sadness and struggles. Our triggers and our wounds. They impact how resourced and resilient we feel, so sometimes we need to adjust our expectations of ourselves as changemakers in response. I did not. I separated myself into Katie with the sick brother and Katie at The Resilience Project. And the dissonance led to my body breaking down.

I learned that saying yes to grief did not end me. Prior to this experience, Grief didn't get a plate of food at my Emotional Banquet. Why? Firstly, because exploring feelings of grief could potentially destabilize me, which would have negatively impacted my ability to keep going and keep productivity high. Secondly, my privilege of not living on the front lines of the climate crisis invalidated my right to feel Grief – it wasn't mine to hold. Thirdly, speaking with Grief was a waste of time, and time needed to be spent on the urgent matter at hand: environmental cataclysm. Finally, Grief sounded sad. Sadness wasn't something I wanted to cultivate in my life. So, Grief was banished to the back room and her plate of food was given instead to Rage and Anger.

The uncertainty of losing Chris saw Grief surface from the back room like a storm. It was not invited into my house as a guest but showed up at the front door with a baseball bat. In doing so, crowds of sorrows violently swept my house.

In saying yes, there were downpours of tears. I had to ask for help a lot and jump off any perceived trajectory I had decided for myself. But something that felt like rock bottom became a stable platform on which to build. I felt the positive by-products of more sleep and hibernation, deeper connections to my friends and closeness to my family. Inside Grief I found purpose. Inside Loss I found appreciation. Only through saying yes to this pain did I surface the next season with the ticklings of motivation, to appreciate my family and my life at a deeper level. It became the backbone for my changemaking. I started seeing Grief as an integral part of changemaking for all the hard and cold bits of wisdom it contains too. Navigating the uncomfortable parts of change – the disillusionment, the headlines, the death – can offer a depth and clarity to the work we are doing, as it did for my personal life. In fact, the real danger of grief, sadness and anxiety lies in avoiding them. These too are welcome here. Or in other words, fight the dragon, get the gold.

The real danger of grief, sadness and anxiety lies in avoiding them.

As a youth activist or a changemaker or an advocate for a kinder world, you often will not have a line-manager or a tutor or even a senior who is directly responsible for you. You won't have someone to tell you that it's time to pull back or take the week off, or that you haven't used your annual holiday allowance. It should therefore be part of your own contract, that when you step into changemaking you sign up for being your own kind and compassionate senior advisor. If you are reading this as a 25-year-old, think of how you would speak to your 18-year-old self and the kindness and grace you'd give them. Then try to embody what your 30-year-old self would say to you now, as a 25-year-old.

What is also important is finding a community of care where you feel able to express the vulnerability that maybe you're not doing okay. We can catch each other's early burnout warning signs and offer each other the permission to rest and step back, which is often so difficult to give ourselves. My own community took care of me at COP26, and my friends cooked dinners, created plans for me and kept me laughing. They sent care packages and cried with me. Like planting crops, what you sow in community returns not just in beauty but feeds you when you've forgotten you were hungry.

Bending and flowing to the rhythms of life is the essence of this stage of Repeat. Learning tools and tips to counter exhaustion may help you in one season and fall short in another. For my own story, my toolbox – rest, joy, professional support – was not enough for 2021. I needed an inventory upgrade. I had to add in the deeper tools that support and sustain me all these years later. This included learning to detach burnout from failure. Considering I was a "resilience practitioner", getting to a point of burnout *again* felt like utter failure, regardless of what was going on in my personal life. I was also expected to be delivering seven burnout workshops during the period of my brother's treatment. I managed to deliver three of them only by making peace with the fact that I would be checking in and disclaiming that I was in fact, very much burned out. Once I started to untangle burntout from failure, I began to shed some of the shame. I also started to feel more human to my peers and colleagues. Showing up as messy and imperfect while leading a personal development course gave everyone else permission to also be somewhere on that journey too. Acceptance became key: accepting that knowledge about burnout did not protect me from it; accepting that being burned out and speaking about burnout did not invalidate me as worthy; accepting that burnout prevention tools couldn't be used to distract myself from pain. And, no matter how in tune I was with myself, there was inescapable pain when considering life without my hero, my brother.

CHAPTER 14:

STOP TRYING TO DIET THE PLANET

I began this book speaking candidly about my eating disorder, and it's also how I will end it. In my early twenties, I had mastered the art of diet failure. It was the time when glossy magazines irresponsibly peddled the latest silver bullet for losing weight. I tried them all. Beyoncé's maple syrup diet – 4/10; calculating points with WeightWatchers – 6/10; even the Cadbury's Curly Wurly diet, which is exactly what it sounds like – 2/10. Like most fad diets, the trajectory became predictable. I'd start feeling empowered. In the first week I was full of energy and resolve, excited to write down my routine and do my supermarket meal plan. Each restrictive meal I ticked off was a win, with the strictness of my intentions rewarded by tipping scales. But by week two or three, I'd be tired, grumpy and hungry. As with most fad diets, weight loss begins to plateau, and I wasn't seeing the weight loss that I would be expecting from such an enormous amount of effort and willpower. Physiologically I'd be lacking the necessary nutrients for adequate functioning. The scales didn't smile back at me, and neither did the woman in the mirror. I grew impatient and my willpower slipped. "One bagel will be fine, right?" would turn into a total food relapse. My body called out for the nutrients and calories it was deficient in and the comfort I'd been deprived of. I'd sit in self-loathing until I found my next dietary method of torture, and the cycle would repeat. Ultimately, nothing ever lasted, and I blamed it on a lack of determination and discipline. I took it as a personal failure and I'd end up heavier than I started, both in weight and in spirit.

Little did I know that buried between the pages of those diet magazines would be a lesson for bettering the planet. Beyond "five ways to beat belly fat", diet culture revealed an integral lesson about human behaviour in that "what feels *good* is sustainable". The diet that will last is the one that makes you feel like your best self. It is the slow and kind lifestyle change that isn't a diet at all – rather, it becomes an integrated approach to your life. For me, that involved a series of fundamental changes. I started to eat intuitively and properly to fuel my body and I began exercising for my mental health rather than to change my aesthetic. I started de-shaming chocolate and ice cream, which alongside my five-a-day, remain core staples of my diet. I resisted the compulsion to sort my days into "green" and "red" days, depending on whether I'd achieved a faint-worthy calorie deficit or eaten three meals and some sugar. "Success" stopped being a physical metric on my body but the days when I stayed faithful to basing my self-worth being on qualities beyond how I look.

Discipline was replaced with radical encouragement. Rather than, "You should eat a salad today because you've eaten like crap this week and you've let yourself down", radical encouragement said, "Hey sweetie, wouldn't it be wonderful to treat your body to some nutrients, spend some you-time slowly and mindfully assembling a full-bodied salad and maybe invite someone over to share it?" Radical encouragement boosts rather than berates.

An integrated lifestyle change might have started as fervent questions about my meal planning, but it ended up with three square meals of self-love and acceptance, with plenty of snacks in between. Food became a doorway to learn to love and respect myself more. These shifts took a long time and involved a huge amount of repeat, growth and relapse, creeping forward and marching back. I learned that it's much easier to skip lunch than to engage in the deeply uncomfortable work of learning to love oneself in any shape or size. Yet the latter has been profoundly important.

What Feels Good Is Sustainable

There are parallels here to bettering the world. Just like a fad diet, there is no one silver bullet to bringing about your desired change. Our campaign may start energizing us with a sense of rigour and purpose, but without seeing the wins or fuelling ourselves appropriately, that energy can start to wane. We begin to question our enormous effort and feel fatigued. We start to have the realization that there is no quick fix, no matter how hard we push.

I began activism with a diet mentality – restriction and discipline. That looked like restricting my carbon emissions as much as possible: no flights, no dairy and no cars. I would say no to holidays, like I'd say no to friends' birthday meals that could compromise my diet. I would be strict – if there was no vegan option, I'd go hungry or go without water rather than buying a plastic bottle of water. At first, I had feelings of both empowerment and taking a stand. I thought I was taking control of what was within my control, living a life of integrity to change the world. But after a while, I started to envy friends going on holiday, just like I grew envious of those eating cake. I became grumpy and alienated from others, unfollowing on social media my dear friends who were travelling the world. While my individual emissions were down, I was starving myself again, but now of joy and connection.

Like dieting, this restriction led to binges. After a particularly difficult break-up I sat at home wondering where the metaphorical ice cream tub was. I decided, "Screw it! I'm going to Portugal" and flew there for a week of sunshine and surf, but unsurprisingly I didn't find the desired healing out there. Any voids within aren't filled by losing weight or hiding in a holiday. I'd packed my sadness in my suitcase. I was still single, still sad, the world was still burning but now I had a tan.

Lifestyle Change Rather Than Fad Diets

Let's use the example of the climate crisis. Controversially, our climate doesn't need a diet. We're taught that decreasing CO_2 emissions is the solution to tackling global warming, but how we get there is equally as important when thinking about long-term effectiveness. If our focus is solely on CO_2 emission reduction, sure, current technologies, innovations and negative emissions technologies can move us toward this goal. At first glance, that's awesome, we did it, we won. But I can't overlook that we'd still exist in a world with widening inequality, a refugee crisis, right-wing extremism and fracturing social relations. Is that winning? Moreover, emission reduction could be effective for a few years, however the capitalist drive for attainment, production and perpetual GDP growth inspires forever striving for "more, more, more". Conspicuous consumption is the act of purchasing and displaying goods and services primarily to signify wealth, social status or economic power, rather than meeting practical needs. Conspicuous consumption, paired with social media, exposes a broader hierarchy of have and have-nots. It is likely that lowering emissions without confronting the psychological drivers of consumption would simply lead to further increased consumption. Emissions would rise again.

The dietary equivalent here is inventing sugar-free alternatives as a solution to increasing rates of obesity – problem solved. Our obesity rates will decline. Not quite. The logic is that fewer calories will result in weight loss, without understanding the psychological drivers behind overconsumption. In reality the advent of zero-calorie drinks and zero-sugar foods has not led to a decline in obesity. The prevalence of severe obesity among US adults increased from 7.7 per cent in 2013–2014 to 9.4 per cent in 2021–2023, highlighting a steady upward trend over the past decade.[43] This is for many reasons, but one is that zero-calorie alternatives can give permission for higher rates of overall consumption – for example, thinking *if the biscuit is sugar free, then I'll have three.*

If we don't simultaneously take stock of our widespread societal values and lifestyle choices, technological change and quick-fix diets have a muted impact. Carbon offsetting can be considered our zero-sugar alternative. Carbon offsetting is the process of companies or individuals offsetting their emissions, often by funding tree planting to remove CO_2 out of the atmosphere. On paper, a victory. In reality, offsetting can legitimize higher rates of consumption overall – for example, thinking *if the flight is carbon free, then I'll take three.* "Offsetting" doesn't address the underlying consumption driver, nor does it interrogate the winners and losers of the offsetting intervention. Offsetting forests has historically displaced or denied access to Indigenous communities. Where plantations exist, monocultures degrade biodiversity. So, we could end up with lower objective emissions but sustained levels of production, ecological degradation and land-grabbing in the Global South. A victory? Or another failed diet?

What the planet needs is a lifestyle change. What I mean by that is that collectively, *societies*, mostly in the Global North and in market economies, need a lifestyle change – one where worth is not rooted in material possessions and we aren't anaesthetizing ourselves with the addictive sugar of the modern-day we call convenience.

Toward Sustainable Changemaking

Changemaking becomes more sustainable when we approach it like a lifestyle change rather than a fad diet. One example here is slow travel, opting where possible for an alternate public transport to flying. Under diet mentality, I saw slow travel and the hours I spent on the train as one of my climate commitments. It was a sacrifice of time, money and productivity. Objectively, it is. What first felt empowering and morally superior, melted into bitter resentment as I sat on a 24-hour bus from Barcelona to London, questioning what on earth the point was. Shifting to a lifestyle-change mindset enabled me to ponder: when do we ever have the time and permission just to do nothing? When can I sit and stare out the window for eight or more hours? If I did this at home on the sofa in my lounge, my housemates would stage an intervention.

Now, slow travel feels like personal maintenance and an investment in myself. If I were to fly, I would move swiftly from one experience to the next without any space or time to reflect. I'd deny myself the opportunity to marinate in the memories, alchemize the learnings and reflect on where I would place this experience in the tapestry of my life. I would instead immediately move on to the next thing, and the next and the next, without drinking in the absolute wonder and diversity of *right now*. Life may feel like it's moving too quickly and passing me by. Intentional space for reflection is almost impossible to come by in our extroverted, high-paced modern world, so I reframed the time spent not flying as "internal activation" time. It felt like a gift rather than a sacrifice. I used the time to journal, to think, to sit, to be. And it felt good. This was still a decision grounded in climate, but this reframe was in service to me, rather than *just* in service to climate.

Fad diets are rooted in the misery of giving something up, whereas making long-term, sustainable changes, while

Changemaking is a life of abundance.

uncomfortable, can come with the joy of abundance. Changemaking is often positioned as a life with limits. This is a diet mentality. But changemaking is a life of abundance. I am a more fully realized person since joining the climate movement. I am a more balanced human: slow travel offers a rare opportunity to escape the rapid pace of the modern world. I am a better cook: plant-based diets will teach you to hunt for flavour in international cuisines. I am a more content person: rejecting conspicuous consumption has forced me to find my worth beyond material success. I have a bigger heart: constantly facing what we are losing and the suffering around the world has made me infinitely more grateful for what I have.

A final key point to "what feels good is sustainable" and the lifestyle change it engenders is unlocking what works for you. Your place doesn't need to be centre stage, and it doesn't even need to be at a march. Where you land might be seasonal. My last half decade of what feels good and authentic has not been spent organizing direct-action work. It has been being backstage, supporting others. This role is no less valid. I'm sure one day I will return to organizing, because campaigns and mass-mobilizations are essential democratic functions and like energetic fault lines for me, but for now my fire is elsewhere. Your place could be delivering speeches, but equally it could be designing compelling communications, making films, hosting book groups or even doing the accountancy for a campaign group. We each have something to give, so find the thing that fits you. Chase the roles and formats that feel nourishing.

Changemaking as a Way of Life

I thought I'd failed at diets, but it turned out that diets failed me. They are set up to fail, so that you buy that next magazine to find another one. You're not the problem, diet culture is. It is not sustainable by design. In a changemaking setting it's probably not that you're not doing enough, it's that active and meaningful participation can be made extraordinarily difficult by government and structures. Only when I reframed my changemaking toward something that felt good did it start to become not just about the end goal but the path I was walking. A new blueprint for changemaking, reframed as a long-term lifestyle change, nourishes not only our campaigns but our relationships, wellbeing, sense of self and life satisfaction.

CHAPTER 15:
REDEFINE WINNING

To truly sustain this work – and ourselves – we need to rethink one of the most powerful forces that shapes our motivation: what it means to win. It can feel counterintuitive, even disheartening, to keep showing up for something as vast and complex as "positive change" without clear, immediate wins. We sign petitions, join marches, change our consumption patterns, have tough conversations with loved ones and still the headlines feel catastrophic. There is a strong temptation to define progress in binary terms: success or failure. A law passes or it doesn't. Your political party wins or loses. We're good or we're screwed. But affecting change, like any deeply human endeavour, lives in the subtleties. Often, the most powerful transformations and cultural shifts are the ones that no one sees.

A Holistic View of Action

The first step in redefined winning is to expand our definition of action, beyond protests, pickets and politics. Typically, action for a positive world has been confined to traditional activism. But what if action could include the large and small acts of hope and humanity that counter the very systems we are trying to transform – systems built on separation, domination and despair? In this framing, radical actions include those that override the defining features of the permacrisis: loneliness, competition, individualism, materialism, convenience, greed, apathy. Actions become offerings to the world we are trying to usher in. In social movement theory, the idea is known as "prefigurative politics", which is simply to be the change you want to see in the world. Actions taken prefiguratively include:

- Showing up to a community event when your instinct is to isolate
- Choosing to stay curious when judgement would be easier
- Having a hard, heartful conversation with a relative about how their opinions might make life feel unsafe for others
- Choosing not to numb out when the news gets heavy
- Gently refusing to disconnect
- Attending a summit, event or conference where you're connecting to something bigger than yourself
- And (one of my strongest resolves) talking to the cashier at the check-out instead of opting for self-service because it might be the first meaningful conversation someone has had the whole day

Through intentional acts of resistance we can disrupt individualism and defy the erasure of non-materiality, such as community, spirituality and love. When we expand our definition of what it means to take action, we simultaneously increase the opportunity for winning. Rather than a win only being something we've pushed for for years, like legalized abortion, it expands to include every interaction of female empowerment you've offered to yourself and others. In this reframe, we can win more frequently. And when we win more often, we feel more hope, because hope is a verb, a doing word.

To win is to feel possibility.

If winning goes beyond protests and pickets, the door opens for more people to participate. If action only looks like shouting en masse (I say this as a shouter myself), most people might assume they're not cut out for it. But if it also includes courageously tabling a justice topic at work or setting up an activism wellbeing support group, or a book group for conservationists, suddenly there's a clearer pathway for engagement. Then the positive feedback loop begins: more winning; more hope; more people offered a way to engage. More people, more winning, more hope. Repeat. To win is to feel possibility, and I'm taken by the transformational power of a heck of a lot more people feeling it.

Our expanded definition of action is not to excuse ourselves from the larger types of action that feel more uncomfortable. We aren't chatting to a stranger to excuse ourselves from decolonizing our campaigns. Expanded winning is not switching off. It's appreciating the manifold forms of positive impact we can pursue. Not only does this expose surfaces for victory, but it illuminates how each and every one of us has the capacity to be a changemaker. Reframing action isn't about lowering the bar but about changing the rules. In this framing, "Well, I've done my bit for today", becomes, "Where else can I do my bit today?" As onlookers we stop shaming others for not doing enough but celebrating them for doing *something*.

The real beauty of this mindset shift is that we won't see it on the news – in fact, we might not see it at all. We don't know how talking to a stranger with curiosity and interest might change the trajectory of their whole day, week or even their life. You don't know the impact of how your decision to slow down and care for your nervous system becomes permission for someone else to do the same. These victories aren't tangible. Change becomes the ripples far beyond our comprehension, which decentres our ego, as we can't as easily claim our virtue or share our action on Instagram. To truly usher in a new world, our changemaking needs to be led by the ecosystem, not by the ego-system. Moments of courage and care matter just as much. Sometimes they matter more.

Reframing both winning and action to be how we show up in the world means that impact doesn't end when the campaign wraps or the grant runs out. It continues in how you move through grief, how you create joy, how you honour boundaries and how you show up – *especially* when no one's watching. Over time, the tools we practise in the eight-week model start to weave into the rest of our lives. We bring this mindfulness into how we parent, lead, rest and relate. We start to ask deeper questions about what kind of world we're creating in our workplaces, our friendships and our personal habits. The work is no longer compartmentalized. So, the real victory, beyond the big and small acts, is integration. Not just policies passed (though we celebrate those), but the healing of our relationship to life itself. What if we redefined changemaking not as conquering, but as alignment? Returning to our values again and again, even when the outcomes are uncertain? What if our metric for success is our ability to stay present, to adapt, to stay in the room when it's hard and to do so with a sustained conviction that we do this because it's right, not because it's easy. These lessons don't just sustain changemaking, they *become* changemaking.

CHAPTER 16: FOUR TYPES OF RESILIENCE

Resilience is not how hard we can brace through challenge or how lightly we can hold global news. It's a multidimensional skillset that allows us to withstand challenges and learn, adapt, grow and spread strength to others. To understand its multifaceted nature, I often draw upon Chris Johnstone's work. He is a friend, resilience specialist and co-author (with Joanna Macy) of *Active Hope*. He outlines four types of resilience that help individuals and communities cope with and adapt to challenges, especially in the context of global crises. His framework helps us see that resilience is not one-size-fits-all, nor something that is a fixed. Rather, akin to the eight-step model, it's something we must perpetually nurture through practice and awareness. He uses the metaphor of bouncing, not just back, but with, forward and outward.

1. Recovery Resilience – Bouncing Back

> *"The ability to return to our previous state after stress or setback."*

This is the resilience most people are familiar with: the capacity to recover after difficulty. It's what we draw on after a hard day, a failure or a loss. It's the part of us that knows how to rest, reset and rebuild.

- **Core question:** How do I restore my energy and wellbeing after adversity?
- **Tools:** Sleep, fun, distraction, nature, self-compassion, supportive relationships, processing sadness.
- **Example:** After a draining campaign or a busy period, you take a week off to rest and reconnect with friends, returning with a clearer mind.

Recovery resilience is vital for avoiding burnout, self-regulation and finding space for ourselves.

2. Adaptive Resilience – Bouncing With

"The capacity to bend and flex without breaking."

This form of resilience helps us stay engaged even when circumstances shift. Adaptive resilience is about adjusting in real time, finding new ways to meet our needs or live our values as conditions change. This is bouncing *with* the pressure, rather than resisting it.

- **Core question:** How can I stay engaged, even as things change?
- **Tools:** Flexibility, curiosity, re-prioritization, creative problem-solving, upgrading our self-care toolkit.
- **Example:** Your campaign loses funding, so you have to rethink strategy and accept the work that won't see the light of day due to the cuts.

Adaptive resilience helps us pivot, rather than collapse. It lets us stay in the game by shifting how we play it.

3. Transformational Resilience – Bouncing Forward

"The ability to grow through difficulty, not just despite it."

This is the most profound and long-term form of resilience. Transformational resilience involves using adversity as a catalyst for growth, allowing experiences to change us for the better.

- **Core question:** What can I learn from this? How might I evolve?
- **Tools:** Reflection, narrative reframing, purpose, therapy, coaching or mentorship.
- **Example:** A climate changemaker hits burnout, re-evaluates their work–life balance and develops a more nourishing model for engagement. Then they share that model with others.

With transformational resilience, we often don't go back to who we were – we move forward as someone wiser, deeper and often more compassionate.

4. Spreading Resilience – Bouncing Outward

"The ability to uplift and support others through our resilience."

This final kind of resilience is about positive contagion. It's what happens when your strength, calm or clarity helps others find their own. When you model recovery or growth, others are more likely to believe it's possible for them too.

- **Core question:** How can my resilience support the resilience of others?
- **Tools:** Storytelling, mentoring, peer support, community building.
- **Example:** After navigating eco-anxiety yourself, you host a support circle where others can share their feelings and explore coping strategies.

Spreading resilience turns personal growth into collective momentum. It's how movements are built, not just on policies or actions but on shared emotional infrastructure.

Putting It All Together

These four types of resilience are not separate stages, but interconnected capacities we can strengthen over time. Feel free to complete the following table in a journal, providing examples of times in your life when you have experienced and practised the four types of resilience.

Type	Metaphor	Core Function	Example from my life
Recovery Resilience	Bouncing Back	Returning to baseline after difficulty	
Adaptive Resilience	Bouncing With	Adjusting to ongoing stress or change	
Transformational Resilience	Bouncing Forward	Growing through adversity, evolving with purpose	
Spreading Resilience	Bouncing Outward	Sharing strength to build collective resilience	

CHAPTER 17:

RETHINKING ACTION AND ANXIETY

After moving through the eight guideposts, we end up back at Act, for the cycle to continue. Action is powerful and necessary for all the reasons I've stated, but action also needs to be considered, self-aware and rooted in a connection to self and others. For the case of climate change, I often see green groups and community leaders suggesting "the solution to anxiety is action" – for example, if you're feeling hopeless, join your local group and start acting. As a catchy idiom, it makes sense. It offers what could be perceived as a "quick fix" for anxiety and it serves to involve more people in necessary change. Double win. But in reality – and we might want to whisper this – action doesn't always ease anxiety from changemaking. In fact, jumping into action can lead to exacerbated ill-health and burnout.

Action needs to be considered, self-aware and rooted in a connection to self and others.

Climate anxiety – or anxiety related to the state of the world – is relational, meaning that it intensifies when we feel people in power aren't doing anything and recedes when we're taking action or witnessing the action of others. You might find that anxiety intensifies when you read a damning headline, see government inaction or perceive widespread societal inertia. You may feel it ease when you take action or participate in a march. Therefore, I see interpersonal dimensions such as alienation, isolation and betrayal as the real meat of the anxiety. So, my first important point is that we simultaneously have a crisis of climate *and* a crisis of connection. Planetary anxiety is uncomfortable, but feeling powerless and holding this giant existential crisis alone is what makes it feel unbearable. Reading statistics on biodiversity loss can be upsetting, but feeling like we are the only one who cares is what can push us to resignation.

Action Alleviates Anxiety

When I was 21, I joined a climate group as a way of lessening my climate anxiety, which presented mostly as anger. In reality, my climate anxiety shot up. The unspoken pressure to know everything about the crisis so I could be a legitimate voice meant that I immersed myself in the science and the statistics. I joined a group of young people doing the same, so we sat in a room where every person knew a different catastrophic fact about planetary degradation. One felt sorrow about the decline of bees, another about the impact of rising sea temperatures on marine life and another that climate change was going to drive up the cost of the pint I was sipping on. Climate anxiety inevitably became contagious, because we were a group of young people who cared deeply about the very intersectional ways in which climate change is the greatest threat of our time. Stoking the fires of urgency left us deprioritizing making real space to talk through all of the sorrow. We'd meet each week to discuss our intended action or campaign, focusing on meeting minutes and agendas to distract from the discomfort. But we all felt exhausted, frustrated and disconnected, and stopping wasn't an option. I have since heard the stories of hundreds of other young people woven together with the same threads that the urgency is so strong we must prioritize action over rest, joy or healthy boundaries. Our narratives tell of martyrdom and exclusion, and talking about our emotions is self-indulgent, a waste of precious time. Feelings of guilt that we're "not doing enough" are both personal and impressed upon us.

Eva came to The Resilience Project in 2021 with a similar experience. She'd been taking climate action since she was 19 and simultaneously seeing a variety of therapists about her climate anxiety. She followed the advice to "take action" and joined a direct-action group in London, infamous for large media moments (and tins of soup). She told me about her campaigns team, which was made up entirely of young people aged 18 to 24 and how they often worked 12 hours or more a day, 6 or sometimes 7 days a week:

> The enormous pressure that exists in youth climate activist spaces is destroying a generation of strong, dedicated young people. We were spurred on by the narrative that our own lives were insignificant in the context of the climate crisis and the urgency of the situation left no time to rest. People were burning out and leaving the movement in huge numbers, while others were so entrenched in the toxic culture that they isolated themselves from friends and family, dropped out of school and disregarded all their own needs. I experienced high levels of anxiety, paranoia, depression, panic attacks and burnout, while others planned their suicides at work.

I've had to change Eva's name as her association with this group has damaged her career prospects. One of the warmest and kindest souls I've worked with, she is having job offers revoked as she's considered a radical extremist. Three schools rejected her teaching placement as they thought she would indoctrinate the children. Her only charge? Getting arrested age 20 for sitting in a street in protest. It breaks my heart and demonstrates the complexity of the psychological turmoil changemakers are facing.

Eva's story is one of many where taking action led to burnout because groups fostered a culture of disconnection and urgency. This results in a phenomenon I observe as "boom and bust", where young people enter movement spaces, inspired to take action, but without adequate tools, knowledge or support for inner and collective resourcing. They might then experience something like burnout and withdraw from the movement entirely. It's a model that some existing groups rely on entirely, burning through people power to maximize frantic and impassioned external action.

Of course, this is not true for *all* movement spaces and things have changed for the better in recent years. I have been part of groups that inspired the eight-week model, where we held firm boundaries, celebrated our identities outside of the fight and gave each other permission to express joy. In fact, for my master's thesis I studied Extinction Rebellion (XR), a group who (beyond their headline-grabbing direct actions) held grief tenders, had wellbeing officers and created utopian scenes in public spaces. I interviewed some members of the climate group to understand their experience. One cited XR as an "antidepressant" and shared that being a part of XR has reaffirmed within her "something I thought I'd lost." Others reflected on the feeling of love, with one who took part in the London protests powerfully stating that, "From the first moment I stepped onto Parliament Square to the second I left Marble Arch the resounding feeling I felt was love."

My second important point is therefore that some action can alleviate anxiety, but some can intensify it as it deepens those relational aspects of loneliness, resignation, exhaustion and hopelessness. If action is to be a "remedy" for anxiety, then we must also turn our gaze toward the culture inside the group taking action. Resisting narratives that shrink space for connection, joy and togetherness can be a radical act. If the relative property of climate anxiety means that it intensifies with government inaction, and it takes a back seat when we feel hopeful and supported and a sense of belonging, the question shifts from: "How do we fix climate anxiety?" to: "How do we build spaces to incubate changemaking that by their very nature make us feel hopeful and supported?"

Then we get to the juicy stuff. The intention after the eight-week model is to start taking action. If we start designing the type of action grounded in our internal landscape and supported by strong communities, it will lead to action that is inspired by imagination and togetherness, rather than urgency and disconnection. We can act in a way that transforms ourselves and our communities at the same time. In doing so, we ease the crisis of connection, and the possibilities expand from reducing carbon emissions to building societies of justice and kinship. My third important point is therefore that taking action is critical and – a big "and" – it can alleviate anxiety from changemaking, *but only when the hub of that action is built on mutual support.*

> Taking action is critical and it can alleviate anxiety from changemaking.

Action Forged by Disconnection

When I was 23, I joined a local climate group in Bristol to blockade the motorway as you enter the city. The intention was to amplify the message of the climate crisis to the masses of commuters on the busiest road in the city. We sang and jumped and cheered to raise awareness – most of us students or people not wearing shoes – while those who were able to get past us screamed, beeped and cussed. Our response to their disquiet was that there was no inconvenience greater than climate change, positioning us on the side of moral righteousness. We hoped to shake people into an understanding that the crisis is here *now* and we need to act (and stop driving cars!) *now.*

The impact was a disaster on three counts. Firstly, targeting commuters created an "us" and "them" divide. It fostered alienation and aggression with no opportunity for meaningful dialogue above the beeps and screams. As an action it felt designed to make us feel better that we were doing *something* rather than nothing, instead of bringing people with power into the conversation. Strike one. Secondly, the march resulted in a three-hour-long standstill on the motorway, with plumes of car engine emissions floating into the communities and neighbourhoods of the people who live next to the motorway. These were poorer communities, the least responsible for the climate crisis, who would experience increased levels of air pollution in the following weeks. Strike two. On top of that, we pissed off thousands of people. Strike three.

Rather than be swallowed by shame, this action gave me a lot to reflect on. My intention was to raise awareness, but my impact was to negatively impact thousands of people, increase emissions into a poorer neighbourhood and sully the climate movement's reputation. By sitting on the road, we positioned ourselves as the morally pious and literally forged a block between our group and the general population. I borrow from the decolonial movement that *intention* and *impact* are not the same thing. Focus on intention foregrounds the perpetrator, focus on impact foregrounds those impacted. Rather than bringing people into the conversation (intention), the impact of our action broke trust between our group and the people of Bristol. It created net-disconnection.

Without pausing to understand the psychological drivers of our campaigns, we risk taking action that leads with ego and creates suffering to ourselves, the movement and others. While climate action can help alleviate climate anxiety, if it's disconnected, pressured or urgency-driven without care for relationships and inner resilience, it can just as easily deepen burnout and despair.

Action alleviates anxiety only when the infrastructure around it also addresses the crisis of connection. Two truths exist at the same time. We desperately need everyone to join our movement club, in every corner, every sector and every space in society, and we deserve to take action which feels joyful, empowering, dare I say it – fun. That's a movement I want to be part of.

"We don't have time for joy and all this woo-woo drama!" Yes, we do. Internal activation is the critical foundation for sustainable external action.

CONCLUSION

"This is the true joy in life, being used for a purpose recognized by yourself as a mighty one. Being a force of nature instead of a feverish, selfish little clod of ailments and grievances, complaining that the world will not devote itself to making you happy. I am of the opinion that my life belongs to the whole community and as long as I live, it is my privilege to do for it what I can. I want to be thoroughly used up when I die, for the harder I work, the more I live. I rejoice in life for its own sake. Life is no brief candle to me. It is a sort of splendid torch which I have got hold of for the moment and I want to make it burn as brightly as possible before handing it on to future generations."[44]

George Bernard Shaw, *Man and Superman*

The truth of this book is that changemaking is both profoundly necessary and profoundly challenging. By stepping into the Arena you are going to get your butt kicked, and moving close to burnout will always be a possibility. If you truly want to create change without burning out, leave your movement, abandon your cause. It's the easiest way to avoid discomfort, pain and loss. But you're stronger than that, more courageous than that and you can do hard things. The challenges we face don't get easier, but we get stronger. Leaving the fight may bring you temporary relief, but you shut yourself off to the most beautiful parts of

The challenges we face don't get easier, but we get stronger.

changemaking: deep kinship with others, connection to something greater than ourselves and a framework for really understanding who we are and what we stand for. What you spend in time, effort and energy you recoup in swathes. To improve the lives of others is a plight so formidable that it will cloak you in a never-ending armour. You will age knowing that you did something. It mattered. Your life mattered. You can't buy, steal or borrow the feeling of living in alignment with your principles. The rewards are lasting, intimate and real. So – do the hard things.

How do we *really* create change without burning out? We make courageous choices. The first is to make an honest enquiry into how you are complicit in your own suffering. The second is to resolve to change. The third is to turn your gaze on systems and structures that perpetuate harm – from historic injustices to toxic workplaces – and make the effort to leave, reform or dismantle them. The fourth is to live in alignment with the learnings you uncover, even when it feels easier to choose comfort and convenience. The fifth is to summon the grace to do it all over again.

In the face of multiple, overlapping crises, it is no longer enough to build campaigns or movements that ignore the emotional, physical and psychological toll on those within them. The staggering rates of burnout illuminate the condition not as a temporary setback but as a warning sign of deeper systemic and psychological misalignments. As the world shifts, changemaking must too. The paradigm shift required bakes inner development into the centre of changemaking, rather than considering it an optional extra. It is one that recognizes self-change, not just self-care, but roots us in a wider collective context. Innertersectional changemaking is a framework that foregrounds inner work *as a vehicle* to broaden our ambitions for change to intersectionality, systems and justice.

Our new changemaking paradigm is human-centred, not goal-oriented, because human-centred activism is activism in its most alive form. Instead of avoiding uncomfortable emotions, it asks us to learn how to create more space to host them. Exhaustion, hopelessness and fatigue are given permission to eat, but not too much and not for too long. The art of hosting requires self-awareness and self-accountability, but also the soft support of others. Tilling our emotional soil creates communities built on mutual aid rather than individual heroism. Born from groups of belonging, connection and support, our activism becomes more spirited, gutsy and inviting. And if we get too close to burnout, our GROWTH Recovery Arc uncovers how we got there and how we'll get ourselves back to baseline. Just like waves in the ocean, we can offer ourselves the grace to perpetually break and begin again.

I hope I've convinced you that changemaking is not only found in metrics and campaign analysis, or even in changes of legislation, but in how we model the values and virtues we wish to bring forward. Each day presents an opportunity to counter the systems we are trying to transform – systems of separation, domination and ego, which all contribute to the crises we see and the wider degradation of the soul. If the latter is robbing us of capable and vitalized agents of change, then walking through the world in a way that contributes to the *reclamation* of the soul is a strong current of impact, one you might never see and never know. So, forage for joy, show up authentically not performatively, and let your actions be guided by the ecosystem, not by the ego-system. In this framing, changemaking isn't a project we take on, but a posture we move from. Radical action becomes less about external conquering or performative success and more about internal alignment. But attitude doesn't equal action, so put this into practice. My hope is that the guideposts laid

Let your actions be guided by the ecosystem, not by the ego-system.

out become less of a textbook and more of a framework for living – the connective tissue that underpins our lives, a way to start tomorrow with more tools, more tenderness and more truth. The guideposts are non-exhaustive. They may not bring all the answers, but they pose a new set of questions: not "How do I feel less tired?" but "How do I feel more alive? How do I resource myself more completely? What change is available to me *now*?"

My twenties have been a journey of learnings, impact and multiple burnouts. Though they were painful and consuming, I am so grateful for them, for they gave me the wisdom that you are never broken – and you are never *not* broken. Burnout illuminated parts of me I didn't want to know and patterns I didn't want to acknowledge. Bringing them to the light and truly listening to them, rather than purging them, engendered a journey not of healing, but of making me whole. Appreciating the wholeness of who we are: the good bits, the battle scars, the deeply conditioned parts and the bits we're always striving to unlearn; the quiet acceptance that we are never not broken. My journey is not over. As I turn 30, my next courageous decision to create change without burning out was made during the writing of this book. After almost six years, and ten years of activism, I have chosen to step back from The Resilience Project as CEO. If change is not a marathon, nor a sprint, but a relay race, then it's time for me to (temporarily) pass the baton. For my own "what next", after a long stint of Act, I'll be beginning my next cycle of Rest, Reset and Repeat to better understand where I can contribute to the movement that is in alignment with who am I now. It's time to install my software updates, find my aliveness and let the ecosystem guide me. Watch this space.

REFERENCES

1 Macy, Joanna & Johnstone, Chris, *Active Hope*, New World Library, Novato (CA), 2022, p.3

2 DataPandas. *Countries Currently at War*. Last updated 24 May 2025. www.datapandas.org/ranking/countries-currently-at-war

3 Shariatmadari, David, "A Year of 'Permacrisis'", *Collins Dictionary – Language Lovers Blog*, 1 November 2022. blog.collinsdictionary.com/language-lovers/a-year-of-permacrisis/

4 Pyle, Edward & Evans, Dani, *Loneliness – What Characteristics and Circumstances Are Associated with Feeling Lonely?* Office for National Statistics, 2018. Retrieved from www.ons.gov.uk/peoplepopulationandcommunity/wellbeing/articles/lonelinesswhatcharacteristicsandcircumstancesareassociatedwithfeelinglonely/2018-04-10

5 Gilder, Lucy, "Climate change: Rise in Google searches around 'anxiety'." *BBC News*, 22 November 2023. www.bbc.co.uk/news/science-environment-67473829

6 Watson, Balogun, Hogg, Joshi, Mugo, Musarurwa, Olude, Wray, Lawrance (2025), "The Resilience Project: The Impact of Peer Support on Youth Climate Anxiety, Social Connectedness and Resilience". (Paper in preparation)

7 Ray, Sarah Jaquette, *A Field Guide to Climate Anxiety: How to Keep Your Cool on a Warming Planet*, University of California Press, Oakland, 2020, p.30

8 Timmermans, Frans, Speech by the Vice President of the European Commission on climate action and youth mobilisation, European Commission, Brussels, 2019
9 Hickman, C, Marks, E, Pihkala, P, Clayton, S, Lewandowski, R E, Mayall, E E, Wray, B, Mellor, C, & van Susteren, L, "Climate anxiety in children and young people and their beliefs about government responses to climate change: A global survey", *The Lancet Planetary Health*, 5(12), 2021
10 Ibid
11 Kamara, Esther Yealie, *Safety for the Youth Climate Movement,* The Urban Movement InnovaKon Fund and Climate Emergency CollaboraKon Group, New York, 2021
12 World Health Organization, "COVID-19 Pandemic Triggers 25% Increase in Prevalence of Anxiety and Depression Worldwide", news release, 2 March 2022, www.who.int/news/item/02-03-2022-covid-19-pandemic-triggers-25-increase-in-prevalence-of-anxiety-and-depression-worldwide
13 Tsui, Tori, *It's Not Just You: How to Navigate Eco-Anxiety and the Climate Crisis,* Gallery Books UK, New York, 2023
14 Foucault, Michel, *Discipline and Punish: The Birth of the Prison*, Penguin, London, 1991
15 Bentham, Jeremy, *Plan of the Panopticon*, 1791, Public domain from Wikimedia Commons
16 Thomas, Leah, *The Intersectional Environmentalist: How to Dismantle Systems to Protect People + Planet,* Souvenir Press, London, 2022
17 World Bank, *Groundswell Part II: Acting on Internal Climate Migration*. Washington, DC: The World Bank, 2021. www.worldbank.org/en/news/press-release/2021/09/13/climate-change-could-force-216-million-people-to-migrate-within-their-own-countries-by-2050

18 Institute for Economics and Peace, *Ecological Threat Report 2020*, Sydney, IEP, 2020. www.zurich.com/media/magazine/2022/there-could-be-1-2-billion-climate-refugees-by-2050-here-s-what-you-need-to-know
19 Oreskes, Naomi & Conway, Erik M, *Merchants of Doubt*, Bloomsbury Press, London, 2010
20 Global Witness, "Standing Firm: Environmental Activists", 13 September 2023. www.globalwitness.org/en/campaigns/environmental-activists/standing-firm/
21 Havel, Václav, *Disturbing the Peace*, Vintage, London, 1991, pp.181–2
22 Frankl, Viktor, *Man's Search for Meaning*, Beacon Press, Boston, 1970, p.31
23 Shulman, Alix Kates, "Dances with Feminists", *Women's Review of Books*, 9(3), December 1991.
24 Butler, Octavia E, *Parable of the Sower*, Four Walls Eight Windows, New York, 1993
25 Panksepp, J, *Affective Neuroscience: The Foundations of Human and Animal Emotions*, Oxford University Press, Oxford, 1998
26 hooks, bell, *All About Love: New Visions*, William Morrow, New York, 2000, p.215
27 Alcoholics Anonymous, "Estimates of AA Groups and Members. AA", 2022. Retrieved from www.aa.org/sites/default/files/literature/SMF-53%20EstimatesofAAGroupsandMembers%20EN%200122.pdf
28 Watson, Balogun, Hogg, Joshi, Mugo, Musarurwa, Olude, Wray, Lawrance (2025), "The Resilience Project: The Impact of Peer Support on Youth Climate Anxiety, Social Connectedness and Resilience". (Paper in preparation)
29 Rumi, Jalalu'ddin, *The Mathnawi of Jalalu'ddin Rumi*, translation by Reynold Nicholson, The Trustees of E.J.W. Gibb Memorial, Luzac, London, 1977

30 World Health Organization, "COVID-19 Pandemic Triggers 25% Increase in Prevalence of Anxiety and Depression Worldwide", news release, 2 March 2022, www.who.int/news/item/02-03-2022-covid-19-pandemic-triggers-25-increase-in-prevalence-of-anxiety-and-depression-worldwide

31 The Children's Society, "Mental Health Statistics." www.childrenssociety.org.uk/what-we-do/our-work/well-being/mental-health-statistics

32 Centers for Disease Control and Prevention (CDC). "Mental Health and Suicide Risk Among High School Students and Protective Factors — Youth Risk Behavior Survey, United States", 2023, MMWR Supplement, Vol. 73 (Suppl-4): pp.79–86, 10 October 2024

33 Tebra Survey. Terba. "Is Self-Diagnosis on Social Media Helping or Hurting People's Health?", *The Intake*, accessed 26 May 2025. www.tebra.com/theintake/medical-deep-dives/tips-and-trends/is-self-diagnosis-on-social-media-helping-or-hurting-peoples-health.

34 Greenfield, Patrick, "Collapsing wildlife populations near 'points of no return', report warns." *The Guardian*, 10 October 2024, www.theguardian.com/environment/2024/oct/10/collapsing-wildlife-populations-points-no-return-living-planet-report-wwf-zsl-warns

35 Weston, Phoebe & Greenfield, Patrick, "Almost 200 people killed last year trying to defend the environment, report finds." The Guardian, 9 September 2024. www.theguardian.com/environment/article/2024/sep/09/almost-200-people-killed-last-year-trying-to-defend-the-environment-report-finds-aoe

36 Davis, Angela Y, in lecture at Southern Illinois University Carbondale, 13 February 2014 (as recalled by attendee Dr. Jonathan Flowers, via a 2024 blog archive)

37 Lorde, Audre, *A Burst of Light: and Other Essays*, Firebrand Books, 1988, "A Burst of Light."

38 Wikimedia Commons, "Original Yerkes-Dodson Graph." commons.wikimedia.org/wiki/File:OriginalYerkesDodson.JPG
39 Butler, Octavia E, *Bloodchild and Other Stories*, 2nd ed., Seven Stories Press, New York, 2005, p.xvii
40 Akomolafe, Bayo, "The Times Are Urgent: Let's Slow Down" 2022. www.bayoakomolafe.net/post/the-times-are-urgent-lets-slow-down
41 Lorde, Audre, *Sister Outsider: Essays and Speeches.* Crossing Press, 1984, p.31
42 Atwood, Margaret, *Author of The Handmaid's Tale Gives Life Advice to Young Leaders*, One Young World, 2024. www.youtube.com/watch?v=mClcEPV1OwA
43 American Beverage Association. "Low- and No-Calorie Beverages Repeatedly Shown to Be an Effective Tool for Weight Loss and Weight Maintenance." *American Beverage Association*, press release. https://www.americanbeverage.org/press-releases/low-and-no-calorie-beverages-repeatedly-shown-to-be-an-effective-tool-for-weight-loss-and-weight-maintenance-2/
44 Shaw, George Bernard, *Man and Superman: Epistle Dedicatory*, 1903.
44 Shaw, George Bernard, *Man and Superman: Epistle Dedicatory*, 1903.

FURTHER RESOURCES

Books

brown, adrienne maree, *Emergent Strategy*, AK Press, Chico (CA), 2017

Burkeman, Oliver, *Four Thousand Weeks: Team Management for Mortals*, Vintage Books, New York, 2022

Dalton-Smith, Saundra, *Sacred Rest: Recover Your Life, Renew Your Energy, Restore Your Sanity*, FaithWords, Brentwood (TN), 2019

Hersey, Tricia, *Rest Is Resistance: A Manifesto*, Little, Brown Spark, New York, 2022

Kimmerer, Robin Wall, *Braiding Sweetgrass: Indigenous Wisdom, Scientific Knowledge and the Teachings of Plants*, Penguin, London, 2020

Loach, Michaela, *It's Not That Radical*, DK, London, 2023.

Macy, Joanna and Johnstone, Chris, *Active Hope: How to Face the Mess We're in with Unexpected Resilience & Creative Power*, New World Library, Novato (CA), 2022

May, Katherine, *Wintering: The Power of Rest and Retreat in Difficult Times*, Rider, London, 2020

Porritt, Jonathon, *Love, Anger & Betrayal*, Mount House Press, 2025

Ray, Sarah Jacquette, *A Field Guide to Climate Anxiety: How to Keep Your Cool on a Warming Planet*, University of California Press, Oakland (CA), 2020

Solnit, Rebecca, *Hope in the Dark: Untold Histories, Wild Possibilities*, Canongate Cannons, London, 2016

Solnit, Rebecca and Lutunatabua, Thelma Young (eds), *Not Too Late: Changing the Climate Story from Despair to*

Possibility, Haymarket Books, Chicago, 2023
Tsui, Tori, *It's Not Just You: How to Navigate Eco-Anxiety and the Climate Crisis,* Gallery Books UK, New York, 2023
Wray, Britt, *Generation Dread: Finding Purpose in the Age of Eco-Anxiety*, Vintage Canada, Toronto, Mississauga and Vancouver, 2023

Websites for Resources and Organizations

Force of Nature – www.forceofnature.xyz
The Nap Ministry – www.thenapministry.com
Polyvagal Theory Resources – www.rhythmofregulation.com
The Resilience Project – www.theresilienceproject.org.uk
Tend: Rest as Resistance Toolkit – www.theblackfeministproject.org/
Unthinkable Resourced Hub – Dr Britt Wray – www.unthinkable.earth
The Work That Reconnects – Joanna Macy – www.workthatreconnects.org
Zen and the Art of Saving the Planet – https://plumvillage.org/courses/zen-and-the-art-of-saving-the-planet

Podcasts

The Force of Nature – www.forceofnature.xyz/fon-podcast
How to Survive the End of the World – Hosted by adrienne maree brown and Autumn Brown
On Dystopia, Hope and Imagination – Margaret Atwood (various recorded talks)
Unlocking Us – Hosted by Brené Brown
We Are the Great Turning – Joanna Macy and Jessica Serrante – resources.soundstrue.com/we-are-the-great-turning-podcast/

ABOUT THE AUTHOR

Katie is an activist, author and founder/Executive Director of the Resilience Project. Named a Global Youth Awards Finalist in 2018 for empowering young people, she has physically mobilised tens of thousands of people for climate action in her early 20s. She founded the Resilience Project, age 24, after seeing little psychological and inner-led support on offer for young people in navigating burnout, climate anxiety and tremendous uncertainty. She has since been invited to share her message on international stages, to Heads of State and CEOs. In the physical world, you'll find her in the Scottish Highlands, where she delights in nature, yoga teaching, wild-swimming and hill-walking.

ACKNOWLEDGEMENTS

This book would not exist without the fierce, brilliant and compassionate people who have held me, challenged me, taught me and walked beside me: Benjamin, Isabel, Emily, Lorna, Georgia, Declan to name a few. An enormous love and thanks to my parents – Judy and Paul – for your unwavering belief and warm love. And, of course, to Chris, my big brother, my biggest champion. You are woven into every line.

Thank you to Graham Maw Christie and my agents Jane Graham Maw and Amy O'Shea, for your patience and support. Thank you to Watkins Publishers and the radiant encouragement of Sophie Blackman. Thank you to the activists I interviewed for this book – Emmanuella Morsi, Rhiannon Hawkins – and those who've inspired the journey – Steve Misati, Grace McMeekin, Samia Dumbuya to name a few. Thank you to Dr Emma Lawrence, Daniella Watson and Dr Britt Wray for orchestrating the research and being great co-conspirators. Thank you to my wonderful team at The Resilience Project who inspire me every day – Abbie, Angela, Matt, Meiyun, Roberta, Judah, Jade, Tala, Hannah. Thank you to Bethan Harris and Esther Maughan-McLachlan for taking a chance on me all those years ago. Thank you to my mentors and coaches – Joey Clifton, Natalie Fee, Jamie Bristow, Marc Jaffrey to name a few.

Mostly I want to acknowledge every young changemaker who trusted me with their story – your courage lives on in these pages. To the Resilience Circles, the collectives and the communities who choose connection over competition, thank you for building spaces where people don't just survive the work, but are transformed by it. You are proof that another way is possible.

To my friends, you remind me that joy, play and softness are sacred. Thank you for giving me room to be human. Thank you to my yoga teacher training cohort, who held my tears when juggling multiple projects all got a bit much. Thank you for sharing that journey with me and to my formidable yoga teacher, Katie White. Thank you profoundly to my community in the Scottish Highlands for only asking me about mountains and never about work.

And finally, to the reader. Thank you for showing up. Whether you arrived here tired, curious, hopeful or heartbroken. May this book be a small offering of solidarity – and a reminder that the work of change belongs to all of us.

INDEX

Note: page numbers in bold refer to diagrams.

WATKINS
1893

The story of Watkins began in 1893, when scholar of esotericism John Watkins founded our bookshop, inspired by the lament of his friend and teacher Madame Blavatsky that there was nowhere in London to buy books on mysticism, occultism or metaphysics. That moment marked the birth of Watkins, soon to become the publisher of many of the leading lights of spiritual literature, including Carl Jung, Rudolf Steiner, Alice Bailey and Chögyam Trungpa.

Today, the passion at Watkins Publishing for vigorous questioning is still resolute. Our stimulating and groundbreaking list ranges from ancient traditions and complementary medicine to the latest ideas about personal development, holistic wellbeing and consciousness exploration. We remain at the cutting edge, committed to publishing books that change lives.